The Cooking Contest Cookbook

More Than 120 Prize-Winning Recipes

❖

Joyce Campagna and
Don Campagna

A Fireside Book
Published by Simon & Schuster
NEW YORK   LONDON   TORONTO   SYDNEY   SINGAPORE

FIRESIDE
Rockefeller Center
1230 Avenue of the Americas
New York, NY 10020

Designed by Ruth Lee
Manufactured in the United States of America

10 9 8 7 6 5 4 3 2 1

Library of Congress Cataloging-in-Publication Data

The cooking contest cookbook : more than 120 prize-winning recipes / [compiled by]
Joyce Campagna and Don Campagna.
     p.   cm.
  Includes index.
   1. Cookery   I. Campagna, Joyce.   II. Campagna, Don.
  TX714.C65437   2000
  641.5—dc21   99-057592

ISBN 0-684-84447-8

To our mothers,

Sindie Rabon Gasque

and

Sadie Jones Campagna

Contents

Introduction

Dear Readers,

For the past ten years I have published *The Cooking Contest Newsletter.* In addition to the latest contests, the newsletter contains recipes that have won recent competitions. What you hold in your hands is a compilation of the best of these award-winning recipes. You will find that what makes this collection unique is that every recipe has been judged by the best palates in the country, not just the taste of one individual.

During the last decade, cooking contests have evolved from events involving a few creative cooks into one of America's fastest-growing hobbies. People from all walks of life have learned how great it feels to hear their name called when the prizes are announced. From honorable mention to grand prize, the exhilaration is addictive. The next thing you know, you are coming up with another new recipe, hoping to feel that thrill again.

Of course, the prizes have increased as well. In an effort to bring in the best new ideas for using their products, sponsors offer everything from training at exclusive culinary schools to good old cash. One million dollars is the top prize in that category. Just think, your favorite dish that everyone raves about may be just what the judges are looking for.

I have also included in this book tips on how to enter and win contests. These have been gleaned from conversations with sponsors, judges, and contestants over the years. One of the wonderful things I have learned is that everyone who participates in these contests finds great pleasure in the success of whoever the winner happens to be. I think that has a lot to do with the kind of person who enjoys preparing and serving good food.

The recipes in this book have all been developed by regular cooks in normal kitchens. Most can be prepared quickly, and all are made with readily available ingredients. The key, though, is taste. From appetizers to desserts, that was the ultimate criterion for inclusion in this volume. Just pick any recipe, and before you know it, you will be serving a delicious dish that has already won thousands of dollars. When you see the pleasure on everyone's face, you, too, will know what it feels like to be a winner.

Sincerely,
Joyce Campagna

The Contest

There are two kinds of contests: cooking contests and recipe contests. The distinction between the two is very simple. Cooking contests require that you show up and prepare a dish. Recipe contests generally require only that you submit your recipe in writing. Cooks that do well in one kind of contest seem to do equally well in the other.

Most cooking contesters prefer the cook-offs because they have a chance to renew friendships formed over years of attending competitions. Usually the sponsor will provide travel and accommodations, so the trip also serves as sort of a cooking vacation. Because these contests are held all over the country, just being a semifinalist can mean a wonderful weekend out of town.

When invited to participate in a cooking contest, expect to be treated royally. The companies involved want everyone to go home with great memories, so they really go out of their way to take care of every need. Events are also planned to make sure you stay entertained. Don't be surprised to find yourself going on a riverboat cruise or rubbing elbows with celebrities.

At contests where participants must prepare their dishes, stoves and grills and ingredients are normally provided. Every effort is made to accommodate requests for specific brand-name products in your recipe, but you should include that information with your submission. If you have a special spoon or bowl you prefer to use, be sure to ask the organizers first.

At the large national cooking contests, participants are taken to the contest site and shown the ingredients they will use to prepare their dish. The cooks are then allowed to satisfy themselves that the food is to their liking. The ovens and ranges are tested to ensure they are working well. These steps always help make the contesters feel more comfortable.

Keep in mind that every contest has a unique set of rules. It is very important to read and follow these directions carefully. It is by looking at the rules closely that you can figure out what kind of recipe the contest really wants. Some may be interested only in thirty-minute dishes, while others will have no time limit. All of them, though, must prominently feature the sponsor's product. In the Appendix (page 281) you will find the rules of three of the most important contests in the country.

Another unique feature of cooking contests is having to perform before an audience. Most of us cook in the privacy of our own kitchen, but in competition, everything has to be done under many watchful eyes. Even at small, local events, contests inspire interest. Very often newspaper and television coverage is present, and frequently winners are interviewed.

To enable participants to stay focused on what they are doing, many contests now provide everyone with a card that is red on one side and green on the other. When red is turned up, no questions are allowed. Green means the cook is open to talking with others. As the contest progresses, fewer and fewer red cards are showing. By the end, the scene looks like a group of friends standing around the stove sharing cooking stories and tips.

Some contests have their own procedures, but in most cases, when a dish is completed and ready for presentation, the contestant is escorted to a receiving area where it is accepted, registered, and passed quickly to the judges. It is during this time, after all the entries are in and before the results are announced, that a lot of friendships are made. With everyone caught up in the excitement of doing their best, contestants pour out the details of their efforts to each other. It is truly a pleasure to be among the most creative and capable cooks in the country and to listen to them talk about their mutual love of food.

When the moment finally arrives for the announcement of the

winner, quiet anticipation is all that can be heard. Then in an instant a name is spoken, and suddenly applause fills the air. For the person called forward there is satisfaction, and for the others there is an appreciation of the talent, skill, and inspiration it took to win. Many contesters say it is the simple recognition of their ability to cook well that they treasure most.

That same reward is available to those who enter recipe contests as well. While the joy of winning may not be shared with a cheering crowd, the excitement is the same when you open an envelope and take out a check with your name on it. You find yourself standing there holding that piece of paper like a diploma. Of the hundreds and thousands of recipes sent in, yours was selected, and there in your hand is the proof.

The process involved in determining the winner of a recipe contest is virtually the same as that used to select cooking contest finalists, the only difference being that a test kitchen is used to prepare the recipes for judging. This element of the contest, though, demonstrates the importance of creating a recipe that can easily be duplicated. Since the entire fate of a recipe contest submission rests on how it looks on paper, it is critically important to write an easy-to-read recipe.

When a recipe contest winner is selected, initial notification frequently takes place by telephone. In confirmation a letter is sent including an affidavit attesting that the rules of the contest have been followed. Upon receipt of your signature, your prize is on the way. All that was required of you was taking the time to write down what you had for supper one night and send it in.

Whether preparing a recipe contest entry or attending a cooking contest, the real prize is the pleasure of creating new ways to enjoy food.

The Contestants

The people who enter cooking contests are the most creative cooks in the country. They are the experimenters. Theirs are the kitchens that new tastes originate in. If you ever have the pleasure of sitting at their table, chances are you will never have exactly the same dish twice. An extra dash of one thing and a splash of something else characterize a good contester.

It is the active creativity of the art of cooking that is a trait of cutting-edge cooks. Just as other people express themselves with clay and paint, contesters apply new layers of flavor to food using unexpected combinations of ingredients. It requires true inspiration to take a favorite old recipe and turn it into new cuisine, and cooking contesters seem to have it.

From a demographic standpoint, contesters do not fit a pattern. Since we all have to cook at one time or another, good cooks come from every walk of life. Among the more successful contesters, there are housewives and molecular scientists, investment analysts and students. What they all seem to share is a real passion for cooking combined with a distinct creative bent.

One of the most difficult things for new contesters to do is learn to be exact. While a dash and a splash might be acceptable for a Saturday night dinner, in order to submit a recipe that others can duplicate, you must actually measure and write down accurate preparation instructions. For a lot of cooks this comes as a real change in behavior. When you are accustomed to throwing things in a pot and having it all come out right, stopping and writing down each step takes getting used to.

Another big adaptation is learning to accept that recipes you are sure will win may not even place. Every contester has tales of wonderful entries that were not chosen. Most also can tell you of having submitted several to a single contest, only to have the one they considered least likely to win selected. It is then that you begin to wonder what you did to catch the judges' eye.

Of course, analysis is one of the many things contesters do well. By keeping up with current food trends, they are able to identify new tastes just as they begin to emerge. Food magazines are a prime source of information, as are newspaper food sections and specialty television shows. It also turns out that many contesters have a lot of cookbooks to which they often refer.

What good contesters are always on the lookout for is another way to serve an old favorite. In a recent contest an imaginative man spread pimiento cheese on pizza crust, cut it into small pieces, and served it as an appetizer. In one easy step a past and a current favorite were combined to create a new party staple.

Most contesters readily admit that the thrill of creating a recipe that other people will actually cook is a great reward in itself. What often does not get talked about as much is the quiet competition that takes place during a contest. If you ever want to see an intense cook, just watch the ones going for a grand prize. While on the outside they may be calm, collected, and willing to take questions from the audience, every move they make around their stove is careful and calculated.

Every measurement is checked twice and every slice or dice is deliberate. Whether the prize is a new kitchen or another blue ribbon, every cook in the contest wants to be able to tell friends and family that he or she won. There are certain bragging rights that come with baking the best biscuits or preparing the perfect pie.

What is so special about cooking contesters is that even though they are involved in the pursuit of recognition for their cooking skills, they never lose sight of the underlying quality of their character. Contesters are people who first and foremost take great delight in giving others pleasure through food. They recognize immediately that even though their recipe may have won, that does not make the other entries any less delicious. In fact, the recipes that finish in less than first place often turn out to be the ones people really cook most often.

It is that willingness to share a great recipe that typifies those who are drawn to contesting. It is also the acknowledgment that even those who do not win eat well.

The Sponsors

Sponsors make possible all the wonderful prizes that contesters win. The prize might be cash or it might be a cruise, but either way, sponsors provide the incentive for contesters to create completely delicious new uses for their products. By sitting down at America's dinner tables, they are able to find out what the ultimate creative consumers are cooking.

Aside from the immediate sales that contests generate, sponsors are really looking for future food trends. In a way, what they are doing is perfect market research. By conducting a contest, a sponsor can mobilize an army of the best cooks in the country whose sole goal is to develop a new way to prepare their product. Sponsors frequently say that they are amazed by, and never would have come up with, the recipes that contesters submit.

It is just such cutting-edge cooking that contesters do every day. Typically, they are what marketing people call experimenters, and this carries over into their kitchens. If you were a grocery store clerk, you would wonder what that customer was going to do with all those unusual ingredients. It wouldn't be at all like guessing from the buns who was going to have hamburgers for supper. The raw ginger, shallots, and teriyaki sauce would have to make everybody at the checkout wonder what the ground beef would ultimately taste like.

What the sponsor hopes is that someone will update an old favorite using their product. A prime example is the tunnel cake a contester created. Filling was added to bundt cake batter, and a brand new classic was born. Even the recent popular use of cilantro can be traced to a winner in the National Chicken Cooking Contest.

Of course, just as there is a National Chicken Cooking Contest, there is a National Beef Cook-Off, as well as other contests of every conceivable kind. A good cook can literally compete in every category from soup to nuts. The competitions range from local to regional and even coast-to-coast television events. What most people do not know is that there is always a great history behind each contest. The prestige of having won a particular contest is more often related to the quality of the previous winning recipes than to the size of the prize.

Still, when the size of the prize does count, the Pillsbury Bake-Off awards the largest prize available—one million dollars. At the first Bake-Off in 1949, Eleanor Roosevelt was the guest of honor and Art Linkletter was master of ceremonies. Now Pillsbury flies in one hundred of the country's best cooks to compete on television. Still, as good as the show is, there is no substitute for experiencing firsthand the pleasures and sensations, the smells and the samples.

As it happens, 1949 was also the year that people began taking their chicken cooking seriously around the Delmarva Peninsula. The contest the poultry producers created began drawing cooks from Delaware, Maryland, and Virginia. In 1971 sponsorship was assumed by the National Broiler Council, and now the contest truly turns out the best chicken recipes to be found in the country. As a matter of fact, what came to be known as chicken fingers was actually introduced years ago at the contest as chicken dippers.

Innovation is also the order of the day at the National Beef Cook-Off. What is especially interesting about their contest is that the most expensive cut of meat is not necessarily the one that wins. Part of the logic behind that may be that the contest was begun by the National Cattle Women. It also appears that their winners tend to feature beef, rather than hide it, in their recipes.

While it is true that the big contests attract the attention, there really are a lot more smaller competitions. Based on the fact that secretly every cook in the community would love to win at the local fair or festival, contests have sprung up everywhere. In Stockton, California, you can be famous for your asparagus, or you can show off your oysters at the St. Mary's, Maryland, annual contest. What is most impressive is that since local bragging rights are on the line at these contests, great care is taken in the selection of a winner. As a consequence, these contests are the source of some of the best recipes in the country.

The Judges

It is quite a responsibility to judge the culinary skills of another. By the time contestants submit their entries, they have practiced making their dishes over and over. To be placed in a position to determine the value of those efforts is humbling. As a judge, you know that someone's dream of hearing his or her name called will come true and someone else's won't.

Given that set of circumstances, the only thing to do is make judgments based strictly on which is the best recipe. After all, that is what the sponsor is looking for. Their best is also what the contestants have prepared. The combination of expectations by both groups puts quite an obligation on the judges. Still, in the final analysis, it is their task to make a decision.

How they arrive at that decision is based on criteria established in the contest rules. Percentages are usually assigned for taste, presentation, creativity, and frequently ease of preparation. While the values will vary from time to time, taste is always most important. Veteran contesters have learned that by paying careful attention to the criteria, they can get a good idea of what it will take to win the contest.

The people who are selected to serve as judges bring every level of education and experience to the table. Often magazine and newspaper food editors are called on, as are culinary arts teachers, well-known chefs, and professional home economists. In some cases, previous winners are asked to help pick their successor. The common factor among them all is their love of good food.

What many people do not know about is the process that determines which recipes will be selected for tasting. While the actual procedures may vary in some contests, professional judging agencies follow rather standard practices. First, great care is taken to ensure that all contests are completely fair. To aid in that matter, recipes are initially screened by an independent agency. They eliminate those that do not follow the format of the contest. They also replace the names of the contestants with numbers on the recipes that are passed on for further judging.

The next step is submission of the recipes to a panel selected by the sponsor. It is at this point that contestants must make their entry stand out from all the rest. Before a dish is chosen for cooking, it has to sound delicious. That is why it is so important to choose a proper name. True to the old adage that the eyes eat first, a descriptive name can make the difference between a recipe that gets read and one that gets tossed. Once a recipe has been chosen, it undergoes actual taste testing.

If the contest is conducted by a company that has its own test kitchen, that is where the recipes will be tried. Under these conditions very strict and rigorous standards are used to ensure that the recipes can be duplicated over and over. Just as often, though, the sponsor may call on staff members to prepare the submissions. What that provides is proof that the dish can be made in everyday kitchens. It is the proper balance between these two that contesters should seek.

Once these preliminary rounds are completed, the job of selecting finalists becomes ever more difficult. By this point all of the recipes that obviously will not work have been eliminated, and what is left is a core group of possible winners. It is important to point out, however, that many delicious dishes never make it past the initial selection process. Sometimes just the sheer number of entries makes it inevitable that good recipes are overlooked.

For those fortunate enough to survive, final judging awaits. In both recipe and cooking contests, that means the judges must try to turn taste into a numerical value. In most contests, to do that, they use a scale of one to ten to rate how each recipe measures up to the criteria the sponsor has established. For example, if taste is to be 60 percent of the total, a recipe can receive anywhere from one to six points. The score in each category is then combined into an overall total. To ensure that an individual cannot unduly influence the outcome, all of the judges' scores are then averaged to determine the final standings.

At large cooking contests where as many as one hundred people may be submitting dishes for consideration, judges really have their work cut out for them. Of course, it is impossible for each of them to taste every dish, so a progressive procedure is used. Once a dish is completed, it is quickly passed to a judge or a table of several judges. If the entry is to their liking, they will recommend that others try it as well.

In the major national contests, there may be as many as thirty individual judges, and in local ones, as few as three. At competitions where appetizers, main courses, and desserts are all included, often judges will taste entries from only one group. Once a category winner is determined, then all of the judges will confer to award an overall prize. With so many factors involved, the difference between first place and honorable mention may be only fractions of a point.

In cooking contests it isn't whether you win or lose but how well you eat.

Tips on How to Enter and Win Cooking Contests

One of the greatest things about cooking contests is that they are scrupulously fair and impartial. Still, there are those who have risen to the top of the contesting world and stayed there. Over the years they have been kind enough to share with me their secrets to consistently winning. Also, judges have confided what it is they are looking for when they are comparing the relative merits of the dishes they are tasting. I have combined all of this knowledge, along with my own experience, into a list everyone can use as a guide to success in this wonderful hobby.

By following the advice of those who have won before, you will greatly improve your chances of creating a winning recipe. The top thirty tips are included in this section, but you will find equally important suggestions from winning cooks scattered throughout the book. The first rule, of course, is to have fun. Cooking contesting is the one thing you can do in your own home with ingredients you already have. It is also something you can share with your family and get immediate feedback from the looks of satisfaction on their faces.

1. **Read and follow directions carefully.** The sponsor has set the rules to fill their needs. Are they searching for a quick and easy recipe utilizing a new product? Do they need a healthy alternative to use for a product that has been on the market for a while? Has the sponsor requested a low-fat, light, or low-sodium recipe? Do they want a special recipe for a special oc-

casion, and decadence is the order of the day? You must figure out from the rules just what it is the sponsor wants, and it is all stated in the rules.

These rules also help the judges get through the hundreds of entries with the most efficiency. The judges will be looking for the information needed in the same location on everyone's entry—any variance can disqualify you. Provide only the information requested and do not include photographs or drawings unless this is stated in the rules. Here you will find the pieces to the puzzle. Study the rules carefully.

2. **Creativity is the key.** Watch food trends and adapt your recipe accordingly. Reading the latest magazines will keep you abreast of what is happening in the food world. They will alert you to new concepts and new food fads. Food trends change constantly, and the people who write about them are quite often the judges who will be judging a contest. If the latest food craze is Mediterranean, for instance, this might be a starting place for you.

Changing a cooking method or style is another area you might want to explore. Do you have a family recipe that has always been fried and has always been an entrée? Consider baking, broiling, or grilling. Have you thought about using this recipe as an appetizer? Don't put limits on yourself—experiment. Don't be afraid to try new methods of preparing old favorites.

3. **Do not use abbreviations.** Write out measurements, such as teaspoon or tablespoon. A misunderstood measurement can ruin an otherwise winning dish. The judges aren't going to spend time trying to figure out confusing and garbled instructions. Be precise and neat. Otherwise, your entry won't make it past the first round, known as the paper-cut.

4. **Simplicity and ease of preparation make winning recipes.** Convenience is stressed in today's cooking. Many contests limit your ingredients and the amount of time required from preparation to the table. Ease of preparation is usually 30 percent of the judging, so keep it simple. New products on our grocery shelves have now combined many flavors, enabling you to eliminate some of the seasonings you would ordinarily use. Tomatoes with basil and chunky salsas are examples. Check your grocery shelves for these fun combinations, and your cooking and prep time can be greatly improved.

5. **Use accurate U.S. measurements.** You must use complete and level

measurements. Never include a pinch or a dash of something. A pinch of salt means different things to different people.

6. **Garnish is very important.** Always remember—eyes eat first. Don't underestimate the importance of presentation and visual appeal. Your dish has to look appetizing and palate tempting.

Think of the last time you ate in a cafeteria. Did you change your choice after you saw how tempting another dish looked?

7. **Feature the contest sponsor's product.** Make the product the star of the recipe. The sponsor wants a good recipe that will sell lots of the product. Use as much as possible, and don't hide it among other things so that no one knows what the idea is. You will be disqualified if you use less than the minimum requirement stated in the rules. Remember—the contest is a promotion to sell products. Create recipes with this in mind.

8. **Analyze recipes that have won previous contests.** If the recipes are available that have won a contest previously, you might want to study them and get a feel for what type of recipe the judges are looking for. Do they lean toward fewer ingredients than you usually use? Do they want the dish on the table in 30 minutes or less? Study the previous winners closely. You may find more information here than you can imagine.

9. **Be sure ingredients used are readily available.** This is a very important rule. Keep in mind that different parts of the country have different tastes; therefore an ingredient that may be considered readily available in the deep South may be unavailable in New York. The sponsor wants a winning dish that will be made often in households across the nation. The ingredients must be available in Any Grocery, USA. Most people don't have time for trips to a specialty store to buy dinner items, so keep this in mind when you are preparing your entries.

10. **Keep up with current diet and health trends.** By reading the current women's magazines, you will note when a new diet or health trend has surfaced. This is very helpful when a contest calls for a heart-healthy dish, for example. You have already done your homework and know what the sponsor has in mind. You won't be tempted to include items that would disqualify you, such as butter or fat.

11. **Write preparation directions in complete sentences.** Here again you should keep in mind the many hundreds of recipes going through the judges' hands. Complete sentences are easy to read and understand. If

the judges can't understand what you mean, your recipe is going to be discarded. Put yourself in the judges' position. When they receive a recipe that is unclear or messy, they are on to the next one. Give yourself a chance—be neat and concise.

12. **List ingredients in order of use.** In making this dish, what is the first ingredient you pick up and place in the preparation bowl? That is the first ingredient you put on your recipe list. So go the second, third, and remaining ingredients. Don't list your ingredients as they come to mind. When the judges read your entry, they want to see a recipe that is organized and easy to follow.

   Here again, you must keep in mind how little time the judges have to decide which recipes to keep from among the hundreds or thousands they have to read. This is vitally important. Be careful listing your ingredients.

13. **Study your favorite cookbook.** This is a good way to teach yourself recipe form. This form will be required in all contests. Some rules change with each contest, but some always stay the same. This is one of the rules that never change. There is one recipe format, and you must submit your entries in this format or be disqualified. The judges look for recipes that meet this criterion, so learn how to do it. It is very simple.

   You may want to look at and study the layout and language. Practice making yours sound like theirs.

14. **Be creative when naming your dish.** You want to make it past the first paper-cut, and to do this *you must get the attention of the judges!* Name your recipe with words that describe the dish in such a tantalizing way that the judges want to taste-test it. Alliteration is a much-used method of naming a dish. With this method you use words that begin with the same letter, as in the title of the recent winner in Mama Mary's Pizza Crust Recipe Contest: Sizzlin' Spicy Scampi Pizza. This name leaves very little to the imagination. We know we are going to get a pizza topped with shrimp scampi that is hot and spicy, and the contestant has combined two of our favorites, pizza and shrimp scampi.

   Puns are another popular method, as in Caribbean Chicken Drums, which recently won $25,000 in the National Chicken Cooking Contest. Rhymes are also a favorite. A $5,000 winner in the National Chicken Cooking Contest was Gingered Jamaican Jerk Chicken. This title just seems to roll off the tongue.

Song titles, titles that refer to ethnic cuisines, and poetry are also used quite often. When you read the names of past winners, you will note that all of them sound tantalizing and beg you to cook them. This is the first place you must grab the attention of the judges, so give it special attention.

15. **Streamline a recipe by combining steps.** The grocery shelves are full of convenience foods, such as canned tomatoes, that have been spiced with almost every kind of seasoning. When a contest states you can use only a certain number of ingredients, you might want to check your grocery shelves to see where you can get added flavor and eliminate an ingredient or two. (This is also a good way to combine ethnic flavors.) Streamline your dish in any way possible, but keep the flavor.

16. **Adapt a recipe for a different occasion.** Do you have a family favorite recipe that is always prepared as a salad? Can it be prepared in another manner, such as a side dish? That excellent cookie recipe you make often; try making it with pureed fruit to eliminate some of the fat and create a lighter entry. Using your imagination is half the fun of contesting.

17. **Create a recipe using ingredients that were once considered unusual but are now readily available in your grocery.** Mango, for instance, can easily be substituted for peaches. Do you remember when everything was garnished with parsley? Look in the produce section of the grocery store and see how many new and exciting items are now available. You might want to buy a book on produce if you aren't familiar with the many different varieties of fruits and vegetables available. Don't be afraid to substitute and try a different flavor. You won't know until you try, and if it doesn't work out, you will learn something that will improve your next attempt.

18. **Consider a dish's versatility.** What requirements are stated in the contest rules? A dish for a tailgate party will be different from a hot entrée. You don't want a dish that requires whipped cream and refrigeration if you are asked for a picnic recipe. Will your dish heat up well if judging is delayed? Is it a dish that the entire family will enjoy, or is it too spicy for the younger or older members of the family? Your recipe must satisfy the palates of all.

19. **Look for ways to enhance flavor.** Ask yourself if a bit more or a bit less of a particular ingredient would help. Some seasonings become stronger with time, so keep this in mind when adding powerful herbs. If you use

more fresh than dried herbs, you will need to know and try out the equivalent dried substitution to make your dish come out right.

20. **Create a new shape or appearance for an old recipe.** A recipe that comes to mind is a $10,000 winner in the recent Pillsbury Bake-Off: Tex-Mex Appetizer Tart. This is basically homemade pimiento cheese placed on top of a refrigerated pie crust, baked, and cut into wedges. An old favorite presented in a new form.

   Use a Bundt pan instead of layers; steam a vegetable salad for a side dish; substitute chicken for beef in a main dish; or make that cookie recipe your family raves about into a cookie pizza and add toppings. There are endless ways to re-create an old favorite.

21. **Include the size of any dish, pots, pans, or casseroles used.** If your recipe is chosen as a semifinalist, it will be tested by home economists, usually in a test kitchen. The size pot or pan you name is the size that will be used, and the wrong size can mean the difference in a recipe that turns out beautifully or one that flops. If your recipe needs to be baked in a glass pie plate instead of metal, make this clear in the instructions. The temperature varies quite a bit.

   This is a very important rule because your finished dish can depend on being prepared in the right size pan. If your recipe needs to be baked in a 9-inch pan, you can imagine what the results will be if it is baked in an 8-inch pan. If you are going to a cook-off, be precise in making your needs known. List everything you will require to produce an outstanding entry.

22. **State the cooking temperatures and time needed to cook the dish.** Work with your temperatures until you have them correct, and state the exact amount of time needed. Give a tip on how to tell when the food is through cooking, such as "bake until golden brown and bubbly" or "sauté vegetables until they are transparent." If you will need a preheated oven, don't forget to include that in your instructions.

23. **Give the number of servings.** Be realistic. "Serves four" is different from "four servings." There are times when someone can eat more than one serving, so make your recipe for four to six servings. This is the amount the judges usually look for when they go through the recipes.

24. **The recipe should have wide appeal.** Recipes should have appeal across the nation and for all lifestyles. If you can create a flavorful dish with less fat, it will be appealing to more people. With all the interest in

heart-healthy dishes today, it is never too early to start eating wisely. The sponsor and the judges will appreciate a dish that is tasty and healthful.

25. **Type or print your recipe.** Almost every contest will give you instructions on where and how to put your name, address, and telephone number on your entry. You will also be told to print or type this information. Your entire entry must be neat, clean, legible, and follow all of the rules.

26. **Double-check the contest rules.** Make sure you have read the rules correctly and understand them. Any variance will disqualify you.

    A good idea is to complete your entry, then put it aside for a day. Sometimes you will find errors that you missed previously and would have disqualified you. If you do find that there is an error, retype or reprint your entry. Neatness goes a long way in making the reading easier for the judges. Remember—they will be looking at a great many recipes, so you want to make sure yours isn't tossed because it isn't legible. Did you put your name and address in the proper corner? Did you include your day and night telephone numbers? Was an entry form required or a UPC? Was a photograph requested or a minimum of the sponsor's product? All of the rules must be honored, or you will be disqualified.

27. **Make a copy of your recipe.** Always make a copy of your recipe for your files. If you are a finalist in a cook-off, you will probably want to practice making your dish several times before the big day. This will make preparing your dish easier and less stressful when you arrive. Usually the press will be milling around asking you questions, so practice will make preparing your dish second nature to you.

28. **Use a separate envelope for each recipe entry.** This rule seldom changes. The rules will state if you can enter as often as you like or are limited to one entry per family. If you are entering more than one recipe, you will want to enter each recipe separately. This makes opening and categorizing the recipes easier.

29. **Your recipe must be original.** This is another rule that seldom changes. When you submit a recipe, you have given copyright to the sponsor. If you enter that recipe again, you are in violation of the copyright law. The sponsor doesn't want to name a recipe a winner if another sponsor claims ownership. In some instances the rules will state that you will be asked to return a prize won in this way.

    An original recipe is the product of one's own mind and is not a copy or imitation. If the recipe is derived from a previously published one, it must have at least four (4) significant ingredients that are different and the method of preparation must be changed to qualify.

30. **Ask yourself the following questions:**

Does the dish taste as good as it could or should?

What can I do to make it taste better?

Is the garnish right? Does it look as good as it should?

Is the aroma good?

Is the texture what it should be?

Will I make this dish on a regular basis?

Appetizers

Antipasto Stuffed Strawberries

1993 CALIFORNIA STRAWBERRY FESTIVAL'S BERRY-OFF

First Place—Appetizers

Roxanne E. Chan

Albany, California

24 large fresh strawberries, hulled

½ cup soft goat cheese

1 teaspoon chopped fresh mint

24 strips (¼ inch wide) prosciutto

Vinaigrette

2 tablespoons olive oil

2 teaspoons balsamic vinegar

1 clove garlic, pressed

¼ teaspoon black pepper

¼ teaspoon grated lemon zest

Garnishes

Shredded spinach, lemon twists, black olives

Use a small melon baller to scoop out the center of each strawberry halfway down. Combine the cheese and mint. Stuff each strawberry, then wrap each horizontally with a strip of prosciutto.

Combine the ingredients for the vinaigrette. Arrange the strawberries on a spinach-lined platter. Drizzle the vinaigrette over the top and garnish the platter with lemon twists and olives.

Makes 24 stuffed strawberries

Oyster Bruschetta "Roma"

13TH ANNUAL NATIONAL OYSTER COOK-OFF
First Place
J. Clairborne Stephens
Middletown, Maryland

2 tablespoons olive oil

½ cup chopped onions

2 tablespoons chopped red bell pepper

2 cloves garlic

½ cup chopped fresh basil

¹⁄₁₆ teaspoon crushed red pepper

24 Maryland oysters, shucked and drained

½ cup seeded, diced tomato

2 tablespoons sliced black olives

2 tablespoons grated Parmesan cheese

½ tablespoon celery salt, or to taste

12 slices (¼ inch thick) French or Italian bread, lightly toasted

¾ cup shredded Vermont white cheddar cheese

Preheat the oven to 400 degrees.

Heat the oil in a medium skillet over medium heat. Add the onions, bell pepper, and garlic. Cook, stirring frequently, 4 minutes. Add the basil and crushed red pepper. Cook 1 minute. Add the oysters and cook, stirring, just until the edges of the oysters begin to curl, 1 to 2 minutes. Remove the skillet from the heat and stir in the tomato, olives, Parmesan, and celery salt.

Mound on bread slices, being sure to have 2 oysters on each. Top with the cheddar and place on a baking sheet. Bake for 5 minutes. Serve hot, warm, or at room temperature.

Makes 12 bruschetta

Popeye's Oysters and Spinach with Bacon Bits

St. Mary's National Oyster Festival
First Place—Outdoor Cookery & Salads
Pat LaBarre
Glen Burnie, Maryland

12 Maryland oysters in the shell
½ cup (1 stick) butter
1 small onion, finely chopped
1 cup finely chopped celery
1 (10-ounce) package frozen chopped spinach, thawed
1 teaspoon Worcestershire sauce
½ teaspoon lemon juice
⅛ teaspoon Tabasco sauce
½ teaspoon salt
1/16 teaspoon black pepper
½ cup grated Parmesan cheese
1 cup crispy bacon bits

Prepare an outdoor grill with medium-hot coals.

Shuck the oysters and return to their shells. Melt the butter in a medium skillet and sauté the onion and celery. Squeeze the spinach dry and add to the onion and celery. Sauté 2 minutes. Add the Worcestershire sauce, lemon juice, Tabasco, salt, and pepper and mix together thoroughly. Top each oyster with the mixture. Sprinkle the Parmesan and bacon bits on top.

Grill over medium-hot coals until the edges of the oysters begin to curl.

Makes 12 stuffed oysters

Baked Brie with Oysters 'n' Pistachios

14TH ANNUAL NATIONAL OYSTER COOK-OFF
Honorable Mention
Shirley DeSantis
East Windsor, New Jersey

Shirley DeSantis
Bethlehem, Pennsylvania

"I like to send entries as soon as possible, since many rules state that if similar entries are received, the first one will be judged. However, I do feel that one can often win with last-minute entries at deadlines. In certain contests (those with various categories) the judges may be looking for something to fill a particular spot in a category. Also, I find it helpful to re-read my recipes a day or so after I type them. I am always surprised, but I do find mistakes. Finally, I am careful to spell out everything from measurements to the size of a can I use in a recipe."

27	Maryland oysters, drained and cut in quarters	1	(14- to 16-ounce) round Brie
3	teaspoons unsalted butter	¼	cup chopped roasted red peppers, drained
¼	teaspoon Old Bay seasoning	1	to 1½ French baguette loaves, sliced
¼	teaspoon black pepper		
⅓	cup chopped unsalted pistachios		

Gently sauté 9 quartered oysters in 2 teaspoons butter in a wok-type pan, adding about two-thirds of the Old Bay seasoning and pepper. Sauté just until the edges of the oysters start to curl. Remove from the heat and stir in about half of the pistachios. Let cool slightly while preparing the Brie.

Insert a sharp paring knife ⅓ to ½ inch from the outside edge of the cheese and trace a ½-inch-deep circle in the top of the cheese. Then use the knife to gently loosen the top rind until it can be removed and saved. With a spoon, scoop out enough of the soft cheese to form a cavity about ½ inch deep. Reserve the scooped-out cheese for another use. Fill the cavity with the oyster mixture. Replace the top rind. Place the Brie on a baking sheet lined with aluminum foil. Cover and refrigerate at least 30 minutes. The cheese can be prepared up to 4 hours ahead.

Preheat the oven to 375 degrees.

Bake the cheese on the center shelf until warm and just softened, 8 to 10 minutes. Remove and let cool 3 to 4 minutes. At the same time, place the remaining butter in a wok-type pan and add the remaining quartered oysters and the red peppers. Sauté, seasoning with the remaining Old Bay and black pepper just until the edges of the oysters curl. Remove from the heat and stir in the remaining pistachios.

To serve: Place the cheese, still on the foil, on a serving dish. Cut the excess foil away. Top with the sautéed oyster mixture. Arrange the sliced French bread around the Brie.

Makes 6 to 12 servings

Majorean Mushroom Tapas with Toasted Almond-Garlic Streusel

1994 BAYS ENGLISH MUFFINS "PASSPORT TO SPAIN" RECIPE CONTEST

Grand Prize

Mary Louise Lever

Rome, Georgia

Almond-Garlic Streusel

1   Bays English Muffin, blended into crumbs (1 cup)

2½ teaspoons olive oil

3   cloves garlic, chopped

¼   teaspoon freshly ground black pepper

¼   cup coarsely chopped almonds

Majorean Mushroom Mixture

2   tablespoons olive oil

⅓   cup finely chopped shallots

1   teaspoon minced garlic

12 ounces mixed mushrooms (preferably button, cremini, shiitake, and oyster), thinly sliced

2   tablespoons dry sherry

½   teaspoon salt

1   tablespoon finely chopped fresh thyme

5   Bays English Muffins, split and lightly toasted

½   cup mascarpone cheese, at room temperature

Thyme leaves for garnish (optional)

To make the streusel: Combine the crumbs, oil, garlic, pepper, and almonds in a large skillet over medium heat. Cook, stirring constantly, until the crumbs and almonds are light golden brown. Spread out on a plate; set aside to cool.

Preheat the oven to 350 degrees.

To make the mushroom mixture: Wipe out the same skillet, add the oil, and heat to medium. Sauté the shallots and garlic until soft, about 2 minutes. Add the mushrooms, sherry, and salt; sauté until the mushrooms are tender, 10 to 12 minutes. Stir in the thyme and continue to cook until most of the liquid evaporates.

Spread each muffin half with mascarpone. Top the mascarpone evenly with the mushroom mixture. Place the tapas on a baking sheet. Bake until hot, about 5 minutes. Spoon the almond-garlic streusel over the mushrooms. Garnish with thyme, if desired.

Makes 10 tapas

Chicken-Broccoli Triangles

PREMIUM YOUNG'N TENDER BRAND
CHICKEN WINNING TASTE RECIPE CONTEST
First Place—Appetizer/Snack Category
Gloria B. Norton
Jacksonville, Florida

1½ pounds (8 to 10 pieces) Premium Young'n Tender Brand boneless, skinless chicken thighs

2 tablespoons oil

¼ crushed red pepper

1 clove garlic, minced

1 (10-ounce) package frozen chopped broccoli, thawed and drained

1 (10¾-ounce) can condensed cream of chicken mushroom soup

¾ cup grated Parmesan cheese

½ cup chopped fresh cilantro

12 sheets frozen phyllo dough, thawed

1¼ cups butter or margarine, melted

Chop the chicken thighs into very small pieces or grind in a food processor. Heat the oil in a large skillet and sauté the chicken, red pepper, and garlic over medium heat until done. Drain; set aside to cool. When cool, add the broccoli, soup, Parmesan, and cilantro. Refrigerate until thoroughly chilled.

Work with one sheet of phyllo dough at a time, keeping the others covered with plastic wrap to prevent drying out. Place one sheet on a dry work surface with a short edge toward you. Brush with melted butter. Fold the bottom up about 3 inches. Cut the dough lengthwise into 6 even strips. Place 1 full teaspoon of chicken filling at the bottom of each strip. Fold into a triangle, folding alternately to the right and to the left until the entire strip of dough is used. Repeat with the remaining dough and filling.

Preheat the oven to 375 degrees.

Brush the top of each triangle with butter and place on an ungreased 15x10x1 baking sheet. Bake for 15 to 20 minutes or until golden brown. Serve hot or cold.

Makes 72 triangles

Cranberry Chicken Wings

CRANEBERRY'S RECIPE CONTEST
Second Prize—Appetizers
Derolyn St. Louis
Carver, Massachusetts

1 (16-ounce) can whole berry cranberry sauce
¼ cup soy sauce
2 cloves garlic, crushed

2 tablespoons brown sugar
½ teaspoon ground ginger
2 pounds chicken wings

Stir together the first 5 ingredients in a saucepan over low heat. Simmer and stir 5 minutes. Toss the chicken wings with the sauce and marinate at least 2 hours in the refrigerator. Remove the garlic.

Preheat the oven to 350 degrees. Bake the wings 1 hour, turning once.

Makes about 20 wings

Tuscan Tuna and White Bean Bruschetta

WOMAN'S DAY/STEEL PACKAGING COUNCIL'S
FASHIONABLE FOODS RECIPE CONTEST
Grand Prize
Edwina Gadsby
Great Falls, Montana

Tuna Mixture

1 (6-ounce) can water-packed tuna
⅓ cup minced red onion
3 tablespoons chopped fresh Italian parsley
1 tablespoon olive oil
2 tablespoons fresh lemon juice
1 teaspoon chopped fresh thyme or ½ teaspoon dried

Bean Puree

1 clove garlic, peeled
1 (15-ounce) can cannellini beans, rinsed and drained
¼ cup chopped drained oil-packed dried tomatoes
¼ teaspoon salt
¼ teaspoon black pepper
20 thin diagonal slices crusty French or Italian bread

To make the tuna mixture: In a small bowl, flake the tuna with a fork. Stir in the remaining ingredients.

To make the bean puree: With the food processor running, drop the garlic through the feed tube and process until chopped. Add the beans and process until smooth. Add the tomatoes, salt, and pepper and pulse just to mix. Scrape into a small bowl.

Preheat the broiler.

Arrange the bread slices in a single layer on baking sheets. Broil 1 to 3 minutes, until lightly toasted. Spread each toast with bean puree, then spoon on some tuna mixture.

Makes 4 to 6 servings

Best-of-the-Border Three-Bean Dip

**WOMAN'S DAY/STEEL PACKAGING COUNCIL'S
FASHIONABLE FOODS RECIPE CONTEST**
First Place—Cold Appetizer/Snack Category
Susan Driscoll
Upper Darby, Pennsylvania

3 scallions, cut in 1-inch lengths
2 tablespoons vegetable oil
2 cloves garlic, peeled
1 tablespoon fresh lime juice
1 tablespoon chili powder
1 tablespoon ground cumin
½ teaspoon salt
¼ teaspoon ground red pepper (cayenne)

1 (15-ounce) can kidney beans, rinsed and drained
1 (15-ounce) can pinto beans, rinsed and drained
1 (15-ounce) can mild green chilies
1 cup reduced-fat sour cream
1 cup mild or medium-spicy salsa
Cilantro sprigs, for garnish
Tortilla chips

In a food processor, process the scallions, oil, garlic, lime juice, chili powder, cumin, salt, and red pepper until the scallions are very finely chopped. Add the beans and chilies; process until well blended but not totally smooth. Spoon half into a medium glass serving bowl. Spread with ½ cup sour cream and ½ cup salsa. Add the remaining bean mixture, spread with the remaining sour cream, and dollop with the remaining salsa. Garnish with cilantro sprigs and serve with tortilla chips.

Makes 8 to 10 servings

Olivita Crostini

WOMAN'S DAY/STEEL PACKAGING COUNCIL'S
FASHIONABLE FOODS RECIPE CONTEST
Winner—Hot Appetizer/Snacks Category
Suzan Ward
Coeur d'Alene, Idaho

1   (4½-ounce) can chopped black olives
½   cup finely chopped pimiento-stuffed green olives
½   cup grated Parmesan cheese
4   tablespoons unsalted butter, at room temperature

1   tablespoon extra-virgin olive oil
2   cloves garlic, minced
¾   cup shredded Monterey Jack cheese
¼   cup minced fresh Italian parsley
1   crusty French baguette

In a medium bowl, stir together the black and green olives, Parmesan, butter, oil, and garlic until well blended. Stir in the Monterey Jack and parsley.

Preheat the broiler.

Cut the baguette into 25 thin slices. Arrange the bread slices on baking sheets and spread some olive mixture on each. Broil 3 to 4 minutes or until the bread is toasted at the edges and the olivita is bubbly.

Makes 4 to 6 servings

White Bean and Bacon Bruschettas

HELLMANN'S/BEST FOODS RECIPE CONTEST
Winner
Roxanne E. Chan
Albany, California

1 (15- to 16-ounce) can white beans, rinsed, drained, and mashed

⅓ cup Hellmann's or Best Foods mayonnaise

2 tablespoons minced red onion

2 tablespoons chopped pitted black olives

1 clove garlic, crushed or minced

½ teaspoon Italian seasoning

½ teaspoon lemon pepper

4 to 6 slices Italian bread, lightly toasted

2 cups fresh spinach leaves, trimmed

4 large tomato slices

8 strips bacon, cooked

¼ cup (2 ounces) shredded mozzarella cheese

In a medium bowl, combine the first 7 ingredients. Place the bread slices on a baking sheet; spread with the bean mixture. Top with the spinach, tomato, and bacon; sprinkle with the mozzarella.

Broil just until the mozzarella is melted and bubbly, 1 to 2 minutes.

Makes 4 servings

Mushroom-Stuffed Brie Baked en Croute

THE MUSHROOM COUNCIL
Third Place
Kristin Love Evans

2 tablespoons butter
½ cup minced onion
8 ounces fresh white mushrooms, chopped (1½ cups)
1 tablespoon dry sherry
½ teaspoon ground nutmeg
¼ teaspoon salt
⅛ teaspoon ground black pepper
1 (17-ounce) package frozen puff pastry sheets, thawed
1 (14- to 17-ounce) wheel of Brie, cut horizontally in half
1 large egg, beaten lightly

In a large skillet, heat the butter until melted. Add the onion; cook, stirring occasionally, until tender, about 6 minutes. Add the mushrooms, sherry, nutmeg, salt, and black pepper; cook until the mushrooms are tender and any liquid evaporates, about 5 minutes. Let cool slightly.

On a lightly floured surface using a rolling pin, roll 2 pastry sheets to ⅛-inch thickness. Place one sheet on a rimmed baking sheet; top with the bottom half of the Brie. Spread the cooled mushroom mixture over the Brie and top with the remaining Brie. Pull the pastry up over the Brie and trim, leaving 1 inch of pastry folded over the Brie. Brush the folded edge with egg.

On the second sheet of pastry, using the diameter of the Brie as your guide, cut out a circle of pastry the same size as the Brie. Place on top of the Brie; press down to seal onto the pastry "rim." Brush all the pastry with egg. Cut a remaining scrap of dough into a mushroom shape. Press on top of the pastry and brush with egg. With the back of a knife, gently score the sides of the pastry with vertical marks, being careful not to pierce the dough. Refrigerate for 15 minutes to set the egg wash.

Meanwhile, preheat the oven to 425 degrees.

Bake the Brie until the pastry is puffed and golden, about 20 minutes. Serve immediately with crackers, if desired.

Makes 20 servings

Soups

Curried Oyster Stew

18TH ANNUAL NATIONAL OYSTER COOK-OFF
Grand Prize
Sally Brassfield
California, Maryland

1	pint Maryland oysters with liquor	2 cups milk
¼	cup butter	½ cup fresh or frozen corn kernels
1	small onion, minced	1 tablespoon dry sherry
1	tablespoon flour	Mashed potatoes
½	teaspoon curry powder	Minced fresh Italian parsley, for garnish
½	teaspoon salt	

Drain the oysters, reserving the liquor. In a 2-quart saucepan, melt the butter. Stir in the onion, flour, curry powder, and salt. Cook for 5 minutes over medium-low heat, stirring frequently. Add the oyster liquid and milk; simmer 2 to 3 minutes. Add the corn and oysters; cook until the edges of the oysters curl. Add the sherry and correct the seasoning. Mound a scoop of mashed potatoes in the center of a large soup plate and place the stew over the potatoes. Garnish with chopped parsley and serve.

Makes 4 servings

Baked Tomato Chowder

PREMIUM SALTINE "BLUE RIBBON" RECIPE CONTEST
First Place—$5,000
Jan Oeffler
Frederic, Wisconsin

Cracker Crust

40 Premium Saltine Crackers, coarsely crushed

½ cup (1 stick) butter or margarine, melted

1 egg, beaten

1 teaspoon garlic powder

Tomato Chowder

8 slices bacon

1 cup chopped zucchini or summer squash

½ cup diced scallions

½ cup julienned green bell pepper

5 cups peeled, seeded, and chopped tomatoes or 1 (29-ounce) can whole tomatoes with juice

2 tablespoons firmly packed light brown sugar

1 teaspoon salt

1 teaspoon dried basil

1 teaspoon dried oregano

1 whole bay leaf

½ teaspoon black pepper

3 drops hot pepper sauce

1 cup shredded Colby-Jack cheese blend

Preheat the oven to 350 degrees. Grease and flour four 1-cup soup or casserole bowls.

To make the crust: Combine the crushed crackers, butter, egg, and garlic powder; mix well. Divide the mixture evenly among the prepared bowls, pressing to form a crust. Bake for 6 to 7 minutes. Leave the oven on.

To make the chowder: Brown the bacon until crisp in a heavy skillet over medium-high heat; remove to paper towels. Reserve 2 tablespoons of the bacon drippings in the skillet. Add the zucchini, scallions, and green pepper; cook 3 to 4 minutes, until tender. Stir in the tomatoes, brown sugar, salt, basil, oregano, bay leaf, black pepper, and hot pepper sauce. Simmer slowly until the tomatoes are tender, 10 to 15 minutes. Remove the bay leaf; crumble the bacon and add to the chowder. Ladle the chowder into the crust-lined bowls and top with the Colby-Jack blend. Bake for 15 minutes.

Makes 4 servings

Mexican Chicken Cheese Soup Ranchero

SARGENTO "CHEESE MAKES THE RECIPE" CONTEST

Grand Prize

Lori Welander

Shelburne, Vermont

12 ounces boneless, skinless chicken breast halves

1 tablespoon fresh lime juice

1 teaspoon chili powder

½ teaspoon ground cumin

3 (14-ounce) cans reduced-sodium chicken broth

3 cups (6 ounces) broken baked corn tortilla chips

2 cups (8 ounces) Sargento Fancy Supreme Shredded Colby-Jack Cheese or 4 Cheese Mexican Recipe Blend

½ cup salsa

½ cup sour cream (optional)

2 plum tomatoes, cut in thin slices (optional)

1 tablespoon chopped fresh cilantro

Place the chicken on a plate; brush both sides with the lime juice; sprinkle the chili powder and cumin evenly over both sides of the chicken; let stand 10 minutes.

Meanwhile, prepare an outdoor grill or preheat broiler.

Grill or broil the chicken 4 to 5 inches from the heat about 5 minutes per side or until cooked through. Let cool; cut into ½-inch pieces.

Meanwhile, bring the broth to a boil in a large saucepan. Add the tortilla chips, cover, and let stand 10 minutes. Puree the mixture in batches in a food processor or blender; return to the saucepan. Stir 1½ cups of the cheese into the broth mixture; cook over medium heat until melted, stirring frequently. Stir in the salsa and chicken; heat through.

Ladle the soup into bowls; top with the sour cream and tomatoes, if desired. Sprinkle with the cilantro and remaining ½ cup cheese.

Makes 6 servings

Mexican Beef and Barley Soup

WORLD BEEF EXPO COOKOFF 1993
Grand Prize
Lloyd ("Roz") Roczniak
Rochester, Minnesota

1 pound ground beef (90 percent lean)

1 small onion, chopped

1 tablespoon olive oil

3 cups reduced-sodium beef broth

2 cups medium or hot chunky salsa

½ cup quick-cooking barley

2 (15-ounce) cans red kidney beans, rinsed and drained

4 tablespoons reduced-fat sour cream

1 teaspoon paprika

In a 12-inch skillet, brown the ground beef and onion in the oil, breaking up with a fork, until the beef is no longer pink; drain. Add the broth, salsa, and barley; bring to a boil. Reduce the heat to medium and cook, uncovered, for 15 minutes.

Add the beans; heat through. Ladle into a soup tureen or individual bowls. Garnish with dollops of sour cream dusted with paprika.

Makes 4 servings

Creamy Broccoli and Wild Rice Soup

35th Pillsbury Bake-Off Contest
$10,000 Winner
Pat Bradley
Rohnert Park, California

1   (10-ounce) package Green Giant Cut Broccoli Frozen in Cheese Flavored Sauce

1   (10-ounce) package Green Giant Rice Originals Frozen White 'n Wild Rice

2   tablespoons margarine or butter

½   cup chopped onion

½   cup chopped celery

½   cup sliced almonds

¼   pound (¾ cup) cubed cooked ham

½   teaspoon dried thyme

½   teaspoon dried marjoram

¼   teaspoon salt

⅛   teaspoon black pepper

3   cups half-and-half or whole milk

Paprika

Cook the broccoli and rice according to package directions; set aside. Meanwhile, melt the margarine in a large saucepan over medium-high heat. Add the onion, celery, and almonds; cook and stir until the vegetables are tender and the almonds are lightly browned. Stir in the broccoli in cheese sauce, rice, ham, thyme, marjoram, salt, and pepper; mix well. Stir in the half-and-half. Cook until thoroughly heated. Do not boil. Ladle the soup into bowls; sprinkle with paprika.

Makes 6 servings

Salads

Kaleidoscope Mushroom Salad

SECOND ANNUAL CYBERSPACE MUSHROOM RECIPE CONTEST
Grand Prize
Louise Ross
Elk Grove, California

20 ounces fresh white mushrooms, sliced (about 6 cups)

Basil Vinaigrette (recipe follows)

8 ounces snow peas, cut diagonally in ¼-inch-wide strips (about 3 cups)

1 cup coarsely chopped watercress

1 cup diced red onion

1 cup corn kernels

½ cup diced pimientos

Radicchio lettuce

Belgian endive

Romaine lettuce (inner leaves)

4 ounces blue cheese, crumbled (about 1 cup)

In a large bowl, marinate the mushrooms in the vinaigrette for 30 minutes. Add the snow peas, watercress, onion, corn, and pimientos; toss gently. If desired, remove a few mushrooms for garnish.

For each serving, in the center of a plate, make a cup using about 3 radicchio leaves. Alternately place endive and romaine lettuce leaves radiating from the cup. Fill each cup with the mushroom-vegetable mixture. Top with blue cheese and garnish the plate with reserved sliced mushrooms. Serve as an appetizer or main dish.

Makes 4 main-dish or 8 appetizer servings

Basil Vinaigrette

⅓ cup chopped fresh basil
2 tablespoons Dijon mustard
1½ teaspoons seasoned salt
¾ teaspoon lemon pepper or black
   pepper

¾ cup vegetable oil
⅓ cup white vinegar
1 tablespoon fresh lemon juice

In a small bowl, combine the basil, mustard, salt, pepper, oil, vinegar, and lemon juice. Stir just before using.

Makes about 1½ cups

Steak Salad Supreme

HANDI-WRAP HAND-ME-DOWN PICNIC RECIPE CONTEST
Grand Prize
Linda Speranza
Phoenix, Arizona

½ cup Italian salad dressing
½ tablespoon capers (drained)
2 teaspoons Dijon mustard
1 pound charcoal-broiled flank steak, thinly sliced

2 ripe tomatoes, chopped
½ small red onion, finely sliced
2 hard-cooked eggs, chopped

Combine the salad dressing, capers, and mustard in a large bowl, stirring to blend. Add the steak and toss with the dressing until well coated. Add the tomatoes, onion, and eggs; gently mix. Cover with Handi-Wrap. Chill at least 2 hours or overnight.

Note: Any cut of steak, grilled or broiled, can be used in this recipe. Sliced roast beef from the deli can also be used. Try broiling an extra steak when you have a barbecue and use it the next day for steak salad.

Makes 4 servings

Marinated Mushroom Salad with Italian Salsa and Gorgonzola Croutons

SECOND ANNUAL CYBERSPACE MUSHROOM RECIPE CONTEST
First Prize
Julie DeMatteo
Clementon, New Jersey

⅓ cup balsamic vinegar

1 tablespoon plus 1 teaspoon Dijon mustard

1 tablespoon minced garlic

½ teaspoon dried thyme, crushed

½ teaspoon dried rosemary, crushed

¼ teaspoon salt

¼ teaspoon coarsely ground black pepper

1 cup olive oil

2 large whole portobello mushrooms, stems removed

12 ounces medium fresh white mushrooms, halved (about 3½ cups)

10 ounces mixed salad greens

1½ cups arugula leaves (1 bunch)

Italian Salsa (recipe follows)

Gorgonzola Croutons (recipe follows)

In a large bowl, whisk together the vinegar, mustard, garlic, thyme, rosemary, salt, and pepper; gradually whisk in the oil. Add the portobello and white mushrooms, turning to coat; set aside for 30 minutes. Drain the marinade from the mushrooms and reserve.

Heat a large skillet over medium-high heat until hot. Sauté the portobellos, then the white mushrooms, turning occasionally, until tender, 4 to 6 minutes. In a large salad bowl, toss the salad greens and arugula with the reserved marinade.

For each serving, on a serving plate, place a quarter of the salad green mixture. Cut half of a portobello into ½-inch-thick slices and place on one side of the plate; arrange a quarter of the white mushrooms on the opposite side. Spoon a quarter of the salsa in the center of the greens and surround with 4 croutons.

Makes 4 servings

Italian Salsa

3 cups diced ripe tomatoes

½ red onion, diced

3 tablespoons minced fresh basil

¼ teaspoon salt

2 tablespoons olive oil

1 tablespoon red wine vinegar

In a medium bowl, combine the tomatoes and onion; toss with the basil, salt, olive oil, and vinegar.

Makes 3 cups

Gorgonzola Croutons

½ cup crumbled Gorgonzola cheese

1 tablespoon olive oil

4 slices (½ inch thick) Italian bread

In a small bowl, combine the Gorgonzola and oil. Spread the mixture over one side of each bread slice. Place in a hot, lightly oiled skillet until the bottoms are lightly toasted and the Gorgonzola is melted, about 2 minutes. Cut each slice into quarters.

Makes 16 croutons

Mediterranean Potato Salad

CHURNY FETA CHEESE RECIPE CONTEST
$5,000 Winner
Helen Conwell
Fairhope, Alaska

6 medium red potatoes, skins on, cubed

2 cups chicken broth

1 clove garlic, minced

2 tablespoons white wine vinegar

½ cup plain yogurt

¼ cup mayonnaise

¼ cup olive oil

1 teaspoon salt, or to taste

1 tablespoon minced fresh dill, or 1 teaspoon dried

1 tablespoon minced fresh oregano, or 1 teaspoon dried

2 tablespoons tiny capers (non-pareils), with juice

8 ounces Churny Feta Cheese, coarsely crumbled

Red lettuce leaves

¼ cup pine nuts, lightly toasted

24 black olives, preferably imported, such as Kalamata

Cook the potatoes in the chicken broth with the garlic until just tender. Drain and reserve the broth for another use. Sprinkle the vinegar on the potatoes and let cool.

Blend the yogurt, mayonnaise, oil, salt, herbs, and capers. Add the feta. Gently fold into the potatoes. Chill overnight, if possible, to blend the flavors. Remove from the refrigerator 1 hour before serving.

Line a platter with the lettuce leaves. Mound the potato salad in the center. Sprinkle with the pine nuts and arrange the olives around the edge.

Makes 8 servings

Grilled Chicken Salad with Asian Ginger Dressing

FETZER WINES GREAT SALAD TOSS 1996
Grand Prize

Nancy Pasquale
Rye, New York

Dressing

4   scallions, roughly chopped

2   cloves garlic, roughly chopped

1½ -inch section fresh ginger, peeled and sliced

⅓   cup seasoned rice vinegar

3   tablespoons toasted sesame oil

½   cup canola oil

Salt and freshly ground black pepper to taste

Salad

1   pound boneless, skinless chicken breast (2 whole or 4 half breasts)

Salt and freshly ground black pepper

1½ pounds mixed salad greens

2   scallions, chopped diagonally

1   large cucumber, peeled and sliced in thin rounds

1   red bell pepper, cut in thin strips

1   orange or green bell pepper, cut in thin strips

2   stalks celery, cut diagonally in thin slices

¾   cup fresh bean sprouts

¼   cup pickled ginger

To make the dressing: Put all the dressing ingredients in a food processor and process using quick pulses until smooth but still leaving some chunkiness. Reserve ½ cup to marinate chicken breasts. Refrigerate remaining ½ cup for at least 3 hours prior to serving.

To make the salad: Season the chicken breasts with salt and pepper and marinate in ½ cup of the dressing at room temperature for ½ hour. Grill or sauté the chicken until done and set aside.

Combine the salad ingredients (except pickled ginger and chicken) in a large bowl and toss with the chilled dressing to coat. Divide into 4 equal servings on large plates. Slice each chicken breast on the diagonal and fan across the top of each plate. Garnish with pickled ginger.

Makes 4 servings

Chicken Salad with Cajun Dressing

PREMIUM YOUNG'N TENDER BRAND
ANNUAL WINNING TASTES RECIPE CONTEST
First Place—Salad Category
Connie Emerson
Reno, Nevada

2 cups Premium Young'n Tender Brand cooked chicken, cut into bite-size pieces

1 cup cooked black beans or 1 (15-ounce) can, rinsed and drained

1 cup cooked white rice

1 cup cooked corn kernels or 1 (11-ounce) can, drained

1 avocado, peeled and cut into chunks

12 cherry tomatoes, halved

8 spinach leaves (optional)

Cajun Dressing

¾ cup olive oil

¼ cup balsamic vinegar

½ cup tomato ketchup

2 cloves garlic, crushed

2 tablespoons minced fresh parsley

1 tablespoon brown mustard

½ teaspoon cayenne pepper

Combine the chicken, black beans, rice, corn, avocado, and cherry tomatoes. Arrange the spinach leaves on salad plates and top with the chicken salad. The mixture may be divided among 4 individual salad plates, with 2 spinach leaves per plate.

To make dressing, combine the oil, vinegar, ketchup, garlic, parsley, mustard, and cayenne in a pint jar. Cover and shake well. Pour the desired amount over the salad.

Makes 4 main-course servings or 6 to 8 side-dish servings

California Asparagus Salad

STOCKTON ASPARAGUS FESTIVAL RECIPE CONTEST
Grand Prize
Joe Mathis
Portola, California

Marinade/Dressing

¼ cup olive oil

½ cup seasoned rice vinegar

Juice of ½ lime

½ teaspoon ground cumin

¼ teaspoon dried oregano

¼ teaspoon black pepper

¼ teaspoon salt

Salad

1¼ pounds fresh asparagus, steamed or simmered until crisp-tender, rinsed with cold water, drained, and cooled

3 boned, skinned, cooked chicken breasts, cut into chunks or bite-size strips

¾ cup mayonnaise (or favorite low-calorie substitute)

½ teaspoon curry powder

6 to 8 large tomatoes

Lettuce leaves

To make the marinade/dressing, combine the first three liquid ingredients. Add the remaining ingredients and blend well.

Reserve 2 to 3 inches of asparagus tips and slice the rest diagonally into ½-inch pieces. Combine the chicken, sliced asparagus, and marinade and stir to coat evenly. Marinate for a minimum of 1 hour (8 to 10 hours is recommended).

Combine the mayonnaise and curry powder, mix well, and refrigerate.

Core the tomatoes, making an 8-point star cut from the top of the tomato almost to the bottom, but not completely through. Open the tomato into a flower (smaller tomatoes may be scooped out to form a bowl). Place the tomatoes on lettuce leaves on individual serving plates, fill each with the marinated chicken-asparagus mixture, and top the mixture with curried mayonnaise. Place 3 or 4 asparagus tips in the curried mayonnaise.

Makes 6 to 8 servings

Pasta & Pizza

Sizzlin' Spicy Scampi Pizza

MAMA MARY'S GOURMET PIZZA CRUST RECIPE CONTEST
Grand Prize—Traditional Category
Gloria Bradley
Libertyville, Illinois

3 tablespoons extra-virgin olive oil

2 cloves garlic, minced

10 ounces uncooked medium to large shrimp, peeled and deveined

1½ tablespoons fresh lemon juice

2 large plum tomatoes, seeded and chopped

¼ cup chopped leek or scallions (white and green part)

2 tablespoons snipped fresh chives

Salt and black pepper to taste

⅓ cup Boursin or cream cheese with garlic and herbs, softened

1 (12-inch) Mama Mary's Gourmet Pizza Crust

¾ cup shredded mozzarella cheese

¼ cup grated Parmesan cheese

2 teaspoons crushed red pepper

Preheat the oven to 450 degrees.

Heat 2 tablespoons of the oil in a large nonstick skillet over medium-high heat. Add the garlic and stir 30 seconds. Add the shrimp and sauté 1 minute. Add the lemon juice and cook until the shrimp are pink and cooked through. Set aside.

In a medium bowl, mix the tomatoes, leek, and 1 tablespoon of the chives. Add the remaining 1 tablespoon oil and season the tomato mixture with salt and pepper.

Spread the Boursin evenly over the crust. Spoon the tomato mixture over the Boursin and top with the cooked shrimp. Sprinkle with the mozzarella, Parmesan, and red pepper. Bake 10 to 12 minutes or until the cheeses are melted. Scatter the remaining tablespoon chives on top of pizza. Cut into slices and serve.

Makes 8 slices

Apple Streusel Dessert

Mama Mary's Gourmet Pizza Crust Recipe Contest
Grand Prize—Dessert Category
Pam Hughes
Olathe, Kansas

1   (12-inch) Mama Mary's Gourmet Pizza Crust
2   tablespoons soft butter

Apple Filling
3   apples, peeled and finely chopped
1   teaspoon ground cinnamon
⅓   cup sugar

Streusel Topping
½   cup (1 stick) butter, at room temperature
⅔   cup sugar
⅔   cup all-purpose flour

Icing
2   tablespoons butter, melted
2   tablespoons milk
1   cup confectioner's sugar
1   teaspoon vanilla extract

Preheat the oven to 400 degrees.

To make the apple filling: Combine the apples, cinnamon, and ⅓ cup sugar; microwave, uncovered, on high for 2 minutes. Set aside.

To make the streusel topping: Cut the butter into the sugar and flour until the ingredients crumble and are well combined. Set aside.

Brush the crust and rim with 2 tablespoons soft butter. Distribute half of the streusel topping over the crust. Spoon all of the apple mixture over the streusel. Top the apples with the remaining streusel mixture. Place the pizza directly on the oven rack. Bake for 10 to 12 minutes.

Combine the ingredients for the icing and drizzle over the warm pizza. Slice and serve.

Makes 8 servings

Pizza-Style Tortilla Stack

LIPTON RECIPE SECRETS CONTEST
Grand Prize
Roxanne E. Chan
Albany, California

Roxanne Chan

Albany, California

Roxanne entered her first contest in 1970. It was a Better Homes and Gardens contest called "Men's Favorite" Recipe. She entered at the urging of her husband, who loved her Turkey Slices with Oyster Sauce. She won Honorable Mention and an 18-volume set of cookbooks. Now Roxanne wins so often that she has been featured in the national media. Her skills seem to have been passed to another generation, given that her young son, Tai-Tien, has already made the winners list of several children's contests.

1   envelope Lipton Recipe Secrets Savory Herb with Garlic Soup Mix

1   (15-ounce) container ricotta cheese

½   cup tomato sauce

10   (6-inch) flour tortillas

1   large green bell pepper, diced

2   (4½-ounce) jars sliced mushrooms, drained

1   (5-ounce) package thinly sliced pepperoni

½   cup pitted ripe olives

1   cup (about 4 ounces) shredded mozzarella cheese

Cherry tomatoes, for garnish (optional)

Chopped fresh Italian parsley, for garnish (optional)

Preheat the oven to 450 degrees.

In a medium bowl, combine the soup mix, ricotta, and tomato sauce.

In a greased 2-quart soufflé or casserole dish, place 1 tortilla. Add layers of the ricotta mixture, green pepper, mushrooms, pepperoni, olives, mozzarella and tortillas, ending with a tortilla. Cover and bake 20 minutes or until heated through. Let stand 10 minutes, then cut into wedges. Garnish, if desired, with cherry tomatoes and parsley.

Makes 6 servings

Lasagna Primavera

NEWMAN'S OWN/GOOD HOUSEKEEPING ANNUAL RECIPE CONTEST
$50,000 Winner
Janet Sutherland
Escondido, California

1 (8-ounce) package lasagna noodles
3 carrots, cut in ¼-inch-thick slices
1 cup broccoli flowerettes
1 cup ¼-inch-thick slices zucchini squash
1 cup ¼-inch-thick slices crookneck squash

2 (10-ounce) packages frozen chopped spinach, thawed
8 ounces ricotta cheese
1 (26-ounce) jar Newman's Own Marinara Sauce with Mushrooms
12 ounces mozzarella cheese, shredded
½ cup grated Parmesan cheese

Bring 3 quarts water to a boil in a 6-quart pan over high heat. Add the lasagna noodles and cook 5 minutes. Add the carrots; cook 2 more minutes. Add the broccoli, zucchini, and crookneck squash and cook the final 2 minutes or until the pasta is tender. Drain well.

Preheat the oven to 350 degrees.

Squeeze the spinach dry. Combine the spinach with the ricotta. In a 3-quart rectangular baking pan, spread one-third of the marinara sauce. Line the pan with lasagna noodles. Put half of each of the vegetables, ricotta mixture, and mozzarella on the noodles. Pour half of the remaining marinara sauce over these layers. Repeat the layers and top with the remaining sauce. Sprinkle with Parmesan.

Place on a 15x10-inch baking sheet that has been lined with foil. Bake, uncovered, for about 30 minutes or until hot in the center. Let stand 10 minutes before serving.

(The casserole can be prepared up to 2 days before baking and refrigerated, covered, until 1 hour before baking. If cold, bake for 1 hour at 350 degrees.)

Serve with Italian bread or rolls, a green salad with Newman's Own Light Italian Dressing, and a bottle of full-bodied red wine.

Makes 8 servings

Hearty Fiesta Cassoulet

NATIONAL PASTA ASSOCIATION'S
"EXCEPTIONAL PASTABILITIES" CONTEST
Grand Prize
Maya Kline
Boise, Idaho

1 pound angel hair pasta, uncooked
2 (14½-ounce) cans tomatoes, diced
2 (15½-ounce) cans black beans
⅔ cup frozen corn kernels
9 ounces smoked sausage, thinly
   sliced

2¼ teaspoons garlic salt
1 teaspoon crushed red pepper
   (optional)
2 tablespoons grated Jack cheese
   (optional)

In a large saucepan, combine the pasta with all of the remaining ingredients except the red pepper and grated Jack. Add 4½ cans water, using a can from the diced tomatoes as a measure. Stir well. Bring to a low boil, cover, reduce the heat, and simmer 10 minutes.

To serve, ladle into soup or chowder bowls. Garnish with the red pepper and Jack, if desired.

Makes 12 servings

Cheese Ravioli-Asparagus Pie

WOMAN'S DAY/CAMPBELL'S CREAM OF ASPARAGUS SOUP
RECIPE CONTEST
Grand Prize
Rosemarie Berger
Jamestown, North Carolina

2 large eggs

1 (10¾-ounce) can condensed cream of asparagus soup

¼ teaspoon black pepper

1 (18-ounce) package frozen ravioli, cooked according to package directions and drained well

1 cup chopped zucchini

2 large plum tomatoes, peeled, seeded, and chopped (1 cup)

2 tablespoons snipped fresh basil leaves, or 2 teaspoons dried

1½ cups shredded mozzarella cheese

Preheat the oven to 375 degrees. Grease a 9-inch pie pan.

In a medium bowl, lightly beat the eggs with a fork. Stir in the undiluted soup and pepper until blended.

Cover the bottom of the pie pan with a single layer of ravioli. Spoon one-third of the soup mixture over the ravioli. Top with half of the zucchini, tomatoes, basil, and mozzarella. Repeat the layers, then top with remaining one-third soup mixture.

Bake 45 minutes or until set in the center and browned on top. Let stand 15 minutes before cutting in wedges.

Makes 4 servings

Thai'd and True Strawberry and Pasta Toss

CALIFORNIA STRAWBERRY FESTIVAL'S BERRY-OFF
First Place—Main Dishes & Vegetables
Roxanne E. Chan
Albany, California

2 cups fresh strawberries, hulled and halved

1 cup shredded Chinese (napa) cabbage

1 cup bean sprouts, cooked 2 minutes, well drained

1 cup shredded spinach leaves

1 bunch red radishes, trimmed and shredded

8 ounces capellini or angel hair pasta, cooked according to package directions

¼ cup chopped fresh cilantro

Dressing

2 tablespoons peanut oil

2 tablespoons chicken broth

2 tablespoons creamy-style peanut butter

1 teaspoon soy sauce

1 teaspoon honey

1 clove garlic, pressed

1 teaspoon finely minced fresh lemon grass

½ teaspoon grated fresh ginger

1 tablespoon lime juice

¼ teaspoon crushed red pepper

½ cup mashed hulled fresh strawberries

Garnish

Chopped roasted peanuts and scallion brushes

Combine the ingredients for the salad in a large bowl. In a saucepan, combine all the ingredients for the dressing except the mashed strawberries and garnishes. Simmer the dressing, stirring, until thickened and smooth. Stir in the strawberries and toss with the salad. Serve immediately with the garnishes.

Makes 4 servings

Jumpin' Jack 'n' Pepper Pizzas

BAYS ENGLISH MUFFINS RECIPE CONTEST
Grand Prize
Marie L. Keir
Chester Springs, Pennsylvania

1 (15-ounce) can black beans, drained

4 cloves garlic, peeled

1 cup seeded, chopped plum tomatoes

3 dashes Tabasco sauce (optional)

6 Bays English muffins, separated into 12 halves

2 cups shredded Monterey Jack cheese with jalapeño peppers

1 red bell pepper, roasted (see Note, page 127), seeded, and chopped

1 yellow bell pepper, roasted, seeded, and chopped

1 green bell pepper, roasted, seeded, and chopped

10 scallions (white and green parts), chopped

12 pitted jumbo black olives, chopped

1 large avocado, peeled, pitted, and chopped

1 tablespoon crushed red pepper

Sour cream

Preheat the oven to 450 degrees.

In a food processor, puree the beans and garlic. Stir in the tomatoes and Tabasco; set aside.

Bake the muffin halves on a baking stone or baking sheet until crisp, about 5 minutes. Remove but leave oven on. Spread a generous spoonful of bean mixture on each muffin half; sprinkle with the Monterey Jack.

In a small bowl, stir together the roasted peppers, scallions, and olives; spoon on top of the cheese. Top each with a few pieces of avocado and sprinkle with red pepper. Bake for 10 minutes or until cheese is bubbly. Serve with a dollop of sour cream.

Makes 6 servings

Deep-Dish Mediterranean Turkey Pizza

TOPSY-TURVY TURKEY RECIPE CONTEST
First Place—Adults
Edwina Gadsby
Great Falls, Montana

1 (10-ounce) can refrigerated ready-made pizza crust

1 pound turkey cutlets, cut in ½-inch-wide strips

2 cloves garlic, minced

½ medium red onion, thinly sliced

2 tablespoons olive oil

1 medium yellow zucchini cut in half lengthwise and sliced

2 medium yellow squash, cut in half lengthwise and sliced

4 medium plum tomatoes, seeded and diced

¼ cup chopped sun-dried tomatoes

1 tablespoon chopped fresh oregano

1 tablespoon chopped fresh basil

2 teaspoons grated lemon zest

1½ cups (6 ounces) shredded mozzarella cheese

1 (2⅓-ounce) can sliced ripe black olives, drained

Preheat the oven to 400 degrees.

Roll the pizza dough into a round approximately 10 inches in diameter. In a 9-inch round cake pan coated with vegetable oil cooking spray, press the dough to cover the bottom and ½ inch up the sides. Prick the bottom all over with a fork.

Bake the dough 8 to 10 minutes, until lightly golden. Leave the oven on.

In a large skillet over medium-high heat, sauté the turkey, garlic, and onion in the oil 3 to 4 minutes, until the onion is soft. Add the zucchini and yellow squash and cook 2 to 3 minutes, until crisp-tender. Stir in the fresh and sun-dried tomatoes, oregano, basil, and lemon zest. Remove from the heat and set aside.

Sprinkle the pizza crust with half of the mozzarella and top with the turkey mixture. Sprinkle the remaining mozzarella and the olives over the turkey mixture. Bake the pizza 4 to 6 minutes, until the cheese melts.

Makes 4 servings

Pasta Rags with Sonoma Tomato Cream Sauce

1997 McCall's/Sonoma Dried Tomato Recipe Contest
Third Prize
Kathleen Chavez
Santa Ana, California

10 Sonoma dried tomato halves

1 cup boiling water

8 ounces lasagna noodles, broken into pieces

1 tablespoon olive oil

8 ounces pancetta, julienned

¼ cup (½ stick) butter

3 leeks (white part only), sliced

1 clove garlic, minced

Salt and pepper to taste

2 cups heavy cream

½ cup grated Asiago or Parmesan cheese, plus extra for garnish

2 tablespoons chopped fresh parsley, plus extra for garnish

Cover the tomatoes with the water in a small bowl to rehydrate for 5 minutes, then drain well. Cut into julienne strips and set aside. Bring a large pot of salted water to a boil. Add the pasta and cook until al dente; drain.

In a large sauté pan, heat the olive oil. Sauté the pancetta in the pan until lightly browned. Remove the pancetta and set aside to drain. In the same pan, melt the butter; sauté the leeks and garlic for 1 minute over high heat. Add the tomatoes, pancetta, salt, and pepper. Sauté for 1 minute longer. Add the cream and let the mixture reduce until thick. Add the cheese, pasta rags, and parsley; toss until well coated. Garnish with more cheese and parsley and serve immediately.

Makes 4 servings

Seafood

Basil-Olive Pesto Stuffed Catfish

CATFISH ON-LINE RECIPE CONTEST
First Prize
Frances Benthin
Scio, Oregon

2 cloves garlic, coarsely chopped

2 cups fresh basil leaves, washed and dried

⅓ cup pine nuts

¼ cup olive oil

½ cup freshly grated Parmesan cheese

¼ cup Kalamata olives, pitted and finely chopped

4 (5-ounce) genuine U.S. farm-raised catfish fillets

Salt and freshly ground black pepper

½ cup dry white wine

1 (4-ounce) container mascarpone cheese (or 4 ounces heavy cream)

½ cup canned roasted red peppers, drained and finely chopped

Parmesan cheese, lemon zest, fresh basil sprigs, Kalamata olives, for garnish (optional)

Preheat the oven to 350 degrees.

To make the pesto, put the garlic, basil, pine nuts, and oil in a blender or food processor. Process until very finely chopped, then stir in the Parmesan and olives.

Season the catfish fillets with salt and pepper. Reserve one-third of the pesto and spread the remaining pesto evenly over the flat side of each fillet. With the pesto inside, roll up the fillets, starting at the tail end, and secure with a toothpick. Stand the rolls in a shallow ovenproof pan without touching each other.

Pour the wine around the fillets and cover the dish with foil. Bake for 20 to 25 minutes or until the fish flakes easily. Remove the fish from the pan and keep warm. Reserve the liquid in the pan.

Bring the reserved liquid to a boil and cook until reduced by half, stirring occasionally. Stir in the mascarpone, roasted peppers, and reserved pesto sauce and adjust the seasoning with salt and pepper, if necessary.

Divide the sauce among 4 plates. Set a fish roll in the center of the sauce. Sprinkle each fillet with Parmesan and garnish with lemon zest, basil sprigs, and olives, if desired.

Makes 4 servings

Grilled Salmon Steaks with Ginger-Chive Sauce

WOMAN'S DAY/BUTTER BUDS RECIPE CONTEST
Grand Prize—$5,000
Teresa Hanna Smith
Santa Rosa, California

4 (1-inch-thick) salmon steaks
1 packet Butter Buds, undiluted
1 teaspoon freshly grated lime zest
½ teaspoon dried dill
¼ teaspoon salt
1 teaspoon vegetable oil

Ginger-Chive Sauce

½ cup reduced-sodium chicken broth
½ teaspoon grated fresh ginger
1 tablespoon fresh lime juice
2 teaspoons snipped fresh chives or thinly sliced scallion greens

Rinse the salmon steaks and pat dry. In a cup, mix half of the Butter Buds with the lime zest, dill, and salt. Sprinkle onto both sides of the salmon and press to adhere.

Heat a ridged cast-iron grill pan or large cast-iron skillet over medium-high heat until hot. Brush the pan with the oil. Add the salmon and cook 4 to 5 minutes per side or until the fish is well browned and just barely opaque near the bone. Remove from the pan to a heated platter.

Meanwhile, make the sauce: Stir the broth, ginger, and remaining Butter Buds in a small saucepan over medium heat until hot and the Butter Buds have dissolved. Remove from the heat and stir in the lime juice and chives. Serve the salmon steaks with small bowls of sauce for dipping.

Makes 4 servings

Caribbean Crunch Snapper with Island Chutney

KRETSCHMER WHEAT GERM
"HEALTHY EATING MADE EASY & DELICIOUS"
RECIPE CONTEST
First Prize—Main Dishes—$1,000
Edwina Gadsby
Great Falls, Montana

⅔ cup Kretschmer wheat germ, any flavor

1½ tablespoons Caribbean jerk seasoning

2 teaspoons grated lime zest

4 (4- to 6-ounce) red snapper fillets

1 egg white

1 tablespoon water

Vegetable oil cooking spray

Chutney

½ cup mango chutney

⅓ cup crushed pineapple in juice, well drained

1 jalapeño pepper, seeded and minced

2 teaspoons chopped fresh mint

2 teaspoons dark rum (optional)

Preheat the oven to 375 degrees. Spray a baking sheet with cooking spray.

In a shallow dish, combine the wheat germ, jerk seasoning, and lime zest; mix well. In a separate shallow dish, beat the egg white and water with a fork until frothy. Dip the fish fillets into the egg white mixture, then into the wheat germ mixture, coating completely. Arrange the fish on the prepared baking sheet. Spray lightly with cooking spray. Bake 20 to 25 minutes, until the fish flakes easily when tested with a fork.

Meanwhile, combine all the chutney ingredients; mix well. Serve the fish with the chutney.

Makes 4 servings

Ranchero Catfish

"FARM-RAISED CATFISH MEALS IN MINUTES" RECIPE CONTEST
Northeastern Winner
Lori Welander
Shelburne, Vermont

4   genuine U.S. farm-raised catfish fillets

1   cup finely crushed tortilla chips

½   teaspoon chili powder

3   tablespoons lime juice

1   tablespoon vegetable oil

1   cup salsa

1   tablespoon chopped fresh cilantro, for garnish (optional)

Preheat the oven to 400 degrees. Lightly grease a baking sheet.

Cut each catfish fillet in half. Rinse in cold water and pat dry with paper towels. Combine the crushed tortilla chips and chili powder in a shallow dish. Mix well. Combine the lime juice and vegetable oil in another shallow dish.

Dip each fillet piece into the lime-oil mixture and then immediately into the seasoned tortilla crumbs to coat. Place on the prepared baking sheet. Sprinkle the fillets with any remaining crumbs and bake until crisp and golden, 15 to 20 minutes, depending on the size and thickness of the fillets. (The catfish should be tender when pierced with a fork in the thickest part.)

Gently warm the salsa; spoon across the center of the catfish fillets. Sprinkle with cilantro, if desired, and serve.

Makes 4 servings

Honey-Thyme Grilled Shrimp

MARVELOUS MARINADE RECIPE CONTEST
Second Place
Gloria Pleasants
Williamsburg, Virginia

Marinade

1   whole garlic head, unpeeled
⅓   cup olive oil
⅔   cup orange juice
¼   cup hot honey mustard
3   tablespoons honey
¾   teaspoon dried thyme, crushed

Kabobs

2   pounds large shrimp, shelled and deveined
1   yellow bell pepper, cut into 1-inch squares and blanched
1   red bell pepper, cut into 1-inch squares and blanched
1   red onion, quartered, separated into chunks

Pint-size Ziploc storage bag
Gallon-size Ziploc storage bag

Preheat the oven to 375 degrees.

Cut off the top one-third of the garlic to expose the cloves. Place the garlic and oil in a small baking dish. Cover tightly; bake 45 minutes. Let cool, then squeeze the garlic pulp from the papery skin. Puree the garlic and oil in a blender with the orange juice, mustard, and honey. Stir in the thyme. Pour ½ cup marinade into a pint-size Ziploc storage bag; seal the bag and refrigerate until serving time.

Pour the remaining marinade, shrimp, peppers, and onion into a gallon-size Ziploc storage bag. Remove the excess air, seal the bag, and turn to coat. Refrigerate 2 hours.

Prepare an outdoor grill with medium-hot coals.

Drain the kabob ingredients well. Discard the marinade and thread the shrimp, peppers, and onion pieces onto metal skewers. Grill on an oiled rack, turning once, for 7 to 10 minutes or until the shrimp are pink. Remove the skewers to a serving tray. With scissors, cut off a tiny corner from the pint-size Ziploc storage bag. Drizzle the sauce over the shrimp and vegetables.

Makes 6 servings

Orange Rosemary Poached Catfish Fillets

"FARM-RAISED CATFISH MEALS IN MINUTES" RECIPE CONTEST
Southeastern Winner
Alma N. Carey
Sarasota, Florida

1   tablespoon cooking oil
2   tablespoons diced red onion
½   teaspoon salt
⅛   teaspoon black pepper
¼   cup fresh orange juice

¼   teaspoon grated orange zest
¼   teaspoon dried rosemary, crushed
1¼   pounds genuine U.S. farm-raised catfish fillets
Orange slices, for garnish (optional)

In a large skillet, heat the oil over medium heat and cook the onion for 5 minutes, until soft but not brown. Sprinkle with the salt and pepper and add the orange juice, orange zest, and rosemary; stir and cook for 1 minute. Add the catfish; lower the heat to medium-low. Cover tightly and cook 8 to 10 minutes, until the fish is opaque.

Remove the catfish to serving plates and spoon the sauce from the skillet over it. Garnish with orange slices, if desired.

Makes 4 servings

Spicy Crab Cakes with Chipotle Aioli

McCall's/Sonoma Dried Tomato Recipe Contest
Grand Prize
Bob Gadsby
Great Falls, Montana

Bob Gadsby

Great Falls, Montana

Bob describes cooking as his favorite pastime and credits his mother's early encouragement as a primary motivating factor. By day he is an agent with the U.S. Customs Service and really enjoys "catching the bad guys." At home he and his wife, Edwina (who also wins a lot of contests), develop quick, easy recipes. Says Bob, "We are busy people and don't have time for complex cooking methods." In the spare time he does have, former firefighter Bob is restoring two old fire engines he owns.

---

15 Sonoma dried tomato halves

1 cup boiling water

½ cup plus ⅓ cup regular or reduced-fat mayonnaise

1 teaspoon minced garlic

1 or 2 chipotle peppers packed in adobo sauce, seeded and minced

1 tablespoon fresh lemon or lime juice

1 egg, beaten

½ cup diced red onion

2 tablespoons chopped fresh cilantro

2 teaspoons Worcestershire sauce

1 pound lump crabmeat or imitation crab, shredded

½ cup fresh bread crumbs

Salt and freshly ground pepper to taste

1 to 2 tablespoons vegetable oil

Cilantro sprigs, for garnish (optional)

Combine the tomatoes and water in a small bowl to rehydrate for 10 minutes. Drain well. Mince 4 softened tomato halves; chop the remaining ones, keeping them separate. To make the aioli, in a small bowl, blend the minced tomatoes, ½ cup mayonnaise, garlic, chipotles, and lemon juice. Cover and refrigerate until serving time.

In a large bowl, combine the chopped tomatoes, ⅓ cup mayonnaise, egg, onion, chopped cilantro, and Worcestershire sauce. Mix in the crab and bread crumbs. Season with salt and pepper. Form into 8 cakes.

Heat the oil in a large nonstick skillet over medium-high heat. Sauté the crab cakes until lightly browned on both sides, about 3 minutes per side. Serve the crab cakes with a dollop of aioli and garnish with cilantro sprigs, if desired.

Makes 4 servings

Glazed Salmon Medallions

**1992 BAYS ENGLISH MUFFINS "ENTRÉE TO THAILAND"
RECIPE CONTEST**
First Place
Gail Gettleson
Bloomfield Hills, Michigan

1   pound skinless salmon fillets
1   (10-ounce) package frozen chopped spinach, cooked and well drained
1   tablespoon butter or margarine
Pinch ground nutmeg
Salt and freshly ground black pepper to taste
4   Bays English muffins, split and lightly toasted
English Mustard Sauce (recipe follows)
8   slices tomato

Preheat the broiler.

Broil the salmon on an oiled broiler pan until barely cooked in the center, 5 to 7 minutes. Leave the broiler on. Combine the cooked spinach with the butter, nutmeg, salt, and pepper. Brush the Bays English muffin halves with the mustard sauce. Top each half with spinach, a tomato slice, and a portion of salmon. Top generously with more sauce; broil 2 minutes, until glazed.

Makes 4 servings

English Mustard Sauce

1   tablespoon dry mustard
½   cup mayonnaise
2   teaspoons bottled steak sauce
2   teaspoons Worcestershire sauce
3   to 4 tablespoons cream

Combine the dry mustard, mayonnaise, steak sauce, and Worcestershire. Gradually mix in cream to the desired consistency.

Makes about ¾ cup

Tortellini-Shrimp Wonderful

1991 SOUTHEAST UNITED DAIRY INDUSTRY ASSOCIATION RECIPE CONTEST

First Place

Sue Gulledge

Springfield, Alabama

- 3 cups fresh cheese tortellini
- ¼ cup (½ stick) butter
- 3 tablespoons fresh lemon juice
- 2 cloves garlic, crushed
- 3 cups medium shrimp, shelled and deveined
- 2 tablespoons dry white wine
- 1 teaspoon dried oregano
- ½ teaspoon salt
- ½ teaspoon black pepper
- ¾ cup reduced-fat sour cream
- ½ cup plain low-fat yogurt
- 6 scallions, sliced
- ½ cup grated Parmesan cheese
- Lemon twists, for garnish
- Oregano sprigs, for garnish

Preheat the oven to 400 degrees. Butter a 2-quart casserole.

Cook the tortellini according to package directions; drain. Melt the butter in a skillet. Add the lemon juice and garlic and cook, stirring, over medium-high heat 2 minutes. Add the shrimp and sauté 3 to 5 minutes. Add the tortellini, wine, oregano, salt, pepper, sour cream, and yogurt. Mix lightly and spoon into the prepared casserole. Top with the scallions and Parmesan cheese. Bake 20 minutes. Garnish with lemon twists and oregano sprigs.

Makes 4 servings

Noilly Prat Napoli Baked Shrimp

1992 NOILLY PRAT/IACP RECIPE CONTEST

First Place—Appetizer

Rene Withstandley

East Dennis, Massachusetts

1 cup Noilly Prat Dry French Vermouth

1 tablespoon fresh lemon juice

2 cloves garlic, minced

1 pound large shrimp, shelled and deveined

Coating

1 cup dry plain bread crumbs

½ cup virgin olive oil

¼ cup chopped fresh Italian parsley

2 cloves garlic, minced

1 teaspoon salt

Freshly ground black pepper to taste

Melted butter or cocktail sauce, for serving

Whisk together the vermouth, lemon juice, and garlic. Add the shrimp and toss. Cover and refrigerate for at least 2 hours or overnight.

Mix together all the coating ingredients. Remove the shrimp from the marinade with slotted spoon, reserving the marinade. Pat the shrimp dry with paper towels. Place in the coating mixture and toss until all the shrimp are well coated.

Preheat the oven to 400 degrees. Butter a 9-inch pie or quiche pan.

Place an inverted custard cup in the center of the pan and arrange the shrimp around the cup. Cover the shrimp with leftover coating. Spoon about half of the marinade mixture over the shrimp. Bake for 10 minutes. Remove the custard cup and place the shrimp under the broiler for 1 minute.

Place the pan of shrimp on a serving dish. Put the custard cup, open side up, back in the center and fill it with melted butter or cocktail sauce.

Makes 4 servings

Scallops Olé

Sargento "Cheese Makes the Recipe" Contest
First Prize—Main Dish—$1,000
Sandra Collins
Wheat Ridge, Colorado

1 green bell pepper, cut in thin rings
1 yellow bell pepper, cut in thin rings
1 red bell pepper, cut in thin rings
¼ cup olive oil
2 cloves garlic, minced
1 cup thick and chunky salsa
1 pound bay scallops, rinsed and drained

1 tablespoon grated lemon zest
1½ cups (6 ounces) Sargento Classic Supreme Shredded Monterey Jack Cheese
Lemon slices, for garnish
Cilantro sprigs, for garnish

Preheat the oven to 400 degrees.

Layer the pepper rings in a 13x9-inch baking dish. Combine the oil and garlic; drizzle over the pepper rings. Bake 20 minutes. Remove from oven; leave the oven on.

Stir the salsa into the pepper rings. Top with the scallops. Sprinkle with the lemon zest and Monterey Jack. Bake 10 to 12 minutes or until the scallops are opaque and the Monterey Jack is golden brown around the edges. Garnish with lemon slices and cilantro sprigs.

Makes 4 servings

Spiced Rubbed Catfish Kabobs with Southwestern Salsa

1992 MISSISSIPPI CATFISH CONTEST
Winner—Summer Category
Roxanne E. Chan
Albany, California

Kabobs

1½ pounds Mississippi farm-raised catfish fillets, cut into 1-inch cubes

3 tablespoons olive oil

2 tablespoons lime juice

½ teaspoon chili powder

¼ teaspoon ground cumin

¼ teaspoon ground coriander

¼ teaspoon black pepper

Salsa

½ cup cooked black beans

1 tomato, diced

¼ cup cooked corn kernels

2 tablespoons chopped fresh cilantro

1 tablespoon sliced almonds

1 scallion, minced

Lime twist, for garnish

Place the catfish cubes in a large bowl. Combine the oil, lime juice, chili powder, cumin, coriander, and pepper in a small mixing bowl. Reserve 2 tablespoons. Pour the remaining mixture over the catfish cubes. Toss to coat. Let the catfish cubes marinate for 20 minutes.

Meanwhile, preheat the broiler.

Thread the marinated catfish cubes onto skewers. Broil 4 inches from heat for 4 minutes. Turn the kabobs and broil 4 minutes more or until the fish is cooked.

Combine the salsa ingredients with the reserved olive oil mixture. Place on a platter and arrange the catfish on top. Garnish with lime twists.

Makes 4 to 6 servings

Tasty Thai Shrimp and Sesame Noodles

NEWMAN'S OWN/GOOD HOUSEKEEPING ANNUAL RECIPE CONTEST
1993 Grand Prize
Beverly Ann Crummey
Brooksville, Florida

1   pound medium shrimp, shelled and deveined

1   (8-ounce) bottle Newman's Own Light Italian Dressing

2   tablespoons chunky peanut butter

1   tablespoon soy sauce

1   tablespoon honey

1   teaspoon grated fresh ginger

½   teaspoon crushed red pepper

1   (8-ounce) package capellini or angel hair pasta

2   tablespoons salad oil

1   tablespoon toasted sesame oil

1   medium carrot, shredded

1   cup chopped scallions

¼   cup chopped fresh cilantro, for garnish

In a medium bowl, mix the shrimp with ⅓ cup Newman's Own Light Italian Dressing. Cover and refrigerate 1 hour. In a small bowl, with a wire whisk or fork, mix the peanut butter, soy sauce, honey, ginger, crushed red pepper, and remaining dressing; set aside. After the shrimp has marinated 1 hour, prepare the capellini as the label directs; drain.

Meanwhile, in a 4-quart saucepan over high heat, heat the salad oil and sesame oil until very hot. Add the carrot and cook 1 minute. Drain off the dressing from the shrimp; discard the dressing. Add the shrimp and scallions to the carrot and cook, stirring constantly, about 3 minutes or until the shrimp are opaque throughout. In a large bowl, toss the hot capellini with the dressing mixture and shrimp mixture. Sprinkle with chopped cilantro.

Makes 4 servings

Glazed Shrimp with Fruit and Nutty Rice Pilaf

CRANEBERRY'S RECIPE CONTEST
First Place—Entrée Category
Frederick J. Lucardie
Tampa, Florida

24 extra-large shrimp, shelled and de-veined

¼ cup vegetable oil

¾ cup black bean and garlic sauce (available at specialty or Asian markets)

½ cup chopped Craneberry's dried cranberries

Rice Pilaf

2 tablespoons butter

1 cup chopped onions

1 cup converted white rice

2 cups hot chicken stock

2 tablespoons soy sauce

1 (5-ounce) package Craneberry's dried cranberries

6 tablespoons pine nuts, toasted

3 tablespoons chopped fresh parsley

Marinate the shrimp in the oil, black bean sauce, and dried cranberries for 1 hour in the refrigerator.

To make the pilaf: Melt the butter in a large saucepan and sauté the onions until translucent. Add the rice, hot chicken stock, soy sauce, and dried cranberries. Bring to a boil, reduce the heat, cover, and simmer for 20 minutes, until the liquid is absorbed. Remove from the heat. Stir in the pine nuts and parsley. Reserve.

Prepare an outdoor grill or preheat the broiler.

Remove the shrimp from the marinade; grill or broil the shrimp until opaque throughout. Serve the shrimp with the rice pilaf and garnish with seasonal fresh vegetables or edible flowers.

Makes 6 servings

Chicken

Spicy Skillet Chicken

FAMILY CIRCLE/FLORIDA CITRUS GROWERS RECIPE CONTEST
Grand Prize
Darol Wetzel
Manhattan, Montana

½   teaspoon citrus pepper
¼   teaspoon ground red pepper
     (cayenne)
½   teaspoon ground ginger
½   teaspoon garlic salt
4   boneless, skinned chicken breast
     halves (about 5 ounces each)

1   tablespoon olive oil
½   cup orange juice
½   cup chopped mango chutney
Orange slices and chives, for garnish
     (optional)

Combine the citrus pepper, red pepper, ginger, and garlic salt in a cup. Sprinkle over both sides of the chicken.

Heat the oil in a large skillet over medium heat. Add the chicken and cook, turning once, 12 minutes or until the chicken is browned on both sides and no longer pink in the center. Remove the chicken from the skillet and keep warm.

Add the orange juice and chutney to the drippings in the skillet; cook, stirring, until thickened slightly, 4 minutes. Spoon some sauce onto 4 serving plates. Place the chicken on the sauce and top with the remaining sauce. Garnish with orange slices and chives, if desired.

Makes 4 servings

Del Monte Chicken 'n' Peaches Picante

DEL MONTE REALITY RECIPES CONTEST
Grand Prize
Gloria Pleasants
Williamsburg, Virginia

Gloria Pleasants

Williamsburg, Virginia

To see Gloria's name on a winners' list is not unusual. It may be that her training as a pharmacist prepared her to understand what makes a delicious recipe. A proud mother, Gloria fondly recalls baking cakes and breads with her own mother before she was old enough to go to school. Her recipe for Del Monte Chicken 'n' Peaches Picante demonstrates in an excellent way how important it is to have a name that will make the judges stop sorting through the stack of entries and read further.

1 (15¼-ounce) can Del Monte Sliced Peaches
4 boneless, skinless chicken breast halves (about 5 ounces each)
Salt and black pepper
1 tablespoon olive oil

½ cup coarsely diced red bell pepper
½ cup thick and chunky salsa
1 tablespoon frozen orange juice concentrate
2 tablespoons chopped fresh cilantro or parsley

Drain the peaches, reserving the liquid, and set aside. Season the chicken with salt and pepper.

In a large nonstick skillet, heat the oil over medium-high heat. Add the chicken and cook 9 to 10 minutes, turning once, until no longer pink in the center. Remove the chicken to a platter.

Add the bell pepper to the skillet, reduce the heat, and cook and stir 2 minutes, until crisp-tender. Add the reserved peach liquid, salsa, and orange juice concentrate to the skillet and bring to a boil, scraping up browned bits from the bottom of the pan. Add the peaches and cilantro and cook and stir 3 minutes, until hot.

Return the chicken to the skillet, along with any juices that have accumulated on the platter. Spoon the sauce and peaches over the chicken until glazed and serve.

Makes 4 servings

Toasted Chicken Salad Wraps

KRETSCHMER WHEAT GERM "HEALTHY EATING MADE EASY & DELICIOUS" RECIPE CONTEST
Grand Prize—$5,000

Ann Chupita
New Brighton, Minnesota

⅓ cup unsalted hulled sunflower or pumpkin seeds

½ cup Kretschmer original toasted wheat germ

1 pound boneless, skinless chicken breast halves

2 tablespoons Creole seasoning blend

1 cup fat-free or reduced-fat mayonnaise

2 cups finely shredded napa or savoy cabbage

½ cup sliced scallions

½ cup diced red bell pepper

6 burrito-size flour tortillas, warmed

Fresh alfalfa sprouts (optional)

In a large nonstick skillet, toast the sunflower seeds over medium-high heat, stirring frequently. Remove from the heat and stir in the wheat germ; transfer to a plate to cool.

Spray the same skillet with cooking spray. Sprinkle the chicken with 1 tablespoon of the Creole seasoning. Cook over medium-high heat 3 to 4 minutes on each side or until no longer pink in the center. Remove the chicken from the skillet; let cool. When cool enough to handle, shred or coarsely chop the chicken.

In a large bowl, combine the mayonnaise and remaining Creole seasoning; mix well. Add the chicken, cabbage, scallions, bell pepper, and wheat germ mixture; mix well.

Spoon the chicken salad down the center of each tortilla, dividing evenly. Fold the sides of the tortilla to the center, overlapping the edges; fold the bottom of the tortilla under, completely enclosing the filling. Spoon alfalfa sprouts into the opening at the top of each wrap. Serve immediately or wrap well and refrigerate up to 8 hours.

Makes 6 servings

Yucatan Chicken with Peach-Avocado Salsa

42ND NATIONAL CHICKEN COOKING CONTEST
Grand Prize
Teresa Hanna Smith
Santa Rosa, California

Teresa Hanna Smith
Santa Rosa, California

Upon learning that she had won, Teresa said, "I can't believe my good fortune. I guess the interest, research, and motivation finally paid off." Of course, the peach tree in her backyard also served as inspiration. She and her husband, Gary, are active members of the ASPCA and find great comfort in the company of their cats. In college Teresa majored in psychology and foreign languages. Both seem to provide her with insight when combining ingredients and selecting a name.

6   boneless, skinless chicken breast halves
1   tablespoon plus 1 teaspoon garlic pepper seasoning
1   orange, juiced
1   lime, juiced
2   tablespoons olive oil
1   teaspoon dried oregano
Peach-Avocado Salsa (recipe follows)
Lime slices, for garnish

Place the chicken in a shallow glass dish; rub all sides with the garlic pepper seasoning. Pour the orange and lime juices over the chicken; drizzle with olive oil. Crush the oregano with your fingers and sprinkle over the chicken. Cover and refrigerate 30 minutes, turning once.

Remove the chicken from the marinade and place in a large nonstick skillet over medium heat. Sauté, turning, about 12 minutes or until lightly browned and a fork can be inserted in the chicken with ease. Serve topped with Peach-Avocado Salsa; garnish with lime slices.

Makes 6 servings

Peach-Avocado Salsa

1   peach, peeled, pitted, and diced
1   small avocado, peeled, pitted, and diced
1   tomato, peeled, seeded, and diced
¼   cup diced jicama

3   tablespoons chopped red onion
2   tablespoons chopped fresh cilantro
¼   teaspoon crushed red pepper
3   tablespoons fresh lime juice
2   teaspoons olive oil

In a medium bowl, mix together the peach, avocado, tomato, jicama, onion, and cilantro.

In a small bowl, whisk together the crushed red pepper, lime juice, and oil. Pour over the peach-avocado mixture, stirring gently.

Makes 3 cups

Basil-Crusted Chicken Oriental

PREMIUM YOUNG'N TENDER BRAND CHICKEN
WINNING TASTE RECIPE CONTEST
Grand Prize
Teresa Hanna Smith
Santa Rosa, California

6 Premium Young'n Tender Brand boneless, skinless chicken breast halves

4 tablespoons butter or margarine, melted

2 tablespoons hoisin sauce

1 tablespoon plus 1 teaspoon Chinese-style hot mustard

⅔ cup Panko Japanese-style bread crumbs or plain dry bread crumbs

3 tablespoons chopped fresh basil or 1 tablespoon dried basil (fresh basil preferred)

2 tablespoons grated Parmesan cheese

Tomato Mustard Cream Sauce

½ cup reduced-fat or regular sour cream

2 tablespoons tomato paste

2 teaspoons Chinese-style hot mustard

1 teaspoon light soy sauce

1 small plum tomato, peeled and diced

Fresh basil and diced plum tomato, for garnish

Preheat the oven to 500 degrees.

Rinse the chicken breasts and pat dry. Combine the butter, hoisin sauce, and mustard in a wide, shallow dish. Mix the bread crumbs, basil, and Parmesan in another shallow dish. Dip each chicken breast in the butter mixture, then in the bread crumb mixture, coating well on all sides. Place in a single layer in a shallow nonstick baking pan. Bake, uncovered, for 15 minutes or until the crumb coating is golden brown and the chicken tests done.

To make the mustard cream: Combine the sour cream, tomato paste, mustard, and soy sauce. Blend well, then stir in one diced tomato. Heat in the microwave on high for 30 seconds, or heat in a saucepan just until warmed.

Spoon the sauce onto a warmed serving platter. Place the chicken breasts over the sauce, or cut the breasts crosswise into thick slices and arrange over the sauce. Sprinkle the chicken with the remaining diced tomato. Garnish with basil and more plum tomato, if desired.

Makes 6 servings

Baked Spicy Pineapple Balinese Chicken

41st National Chicken Cooking Contest
Grand Prize—$25,000
Mary Louise Lever
Rome, Georgia

Mary Louise Lever
Rome, Georgia

Mary Louise's use of gingersnaps in her recipe for Baked Spicy Pineapple Balinese Chicken is a perfect example of the kind of creativity it takes to win the judges' approval. In this case she developed a recipe specifically for the contest and won $25,000 worth of approval. It is interesting to note that she sent it in on the very day of the deadline for entries. When she is not cooking up new recipes, Mary Louise raises money for her local college.

4 boneless, skinless chicken breast halves
3 tablespoons Dijon mustard
½ cup gingersnap crumbs

Spicy Pineapple Sauce (recipe follows)
Red bell pepper strips and basil sprigs, for garnish

Place the chicken between 2 sheets of plastic wrap and gently pound to a uniform thickness; brush with the mustard. Place the gingersnap crumbs in a shallow dish. Add the chicken, one piece at a time, and dredge to coat. Place the chicken in a nonstick shallow baking dish coated with cooking spray and refrigerate 20 minutes.

Preheat the oven to 350 degrees.

Bake the chicken about 20 minutes or until the juices run clear and a fork can be inserted in the chicken with ease.

Divide the Spicy Pineapple Sauce among 4 individual plates and top each with a chicken breast half. Garnish with pepper strips and basil sprigs.

Makes 4 servings

Spicy Pineapple Sauce

1	tablespoon peanut oil	¼	teaspoon ground allspice
1	clove garlic, minced	¼	teaspoon red pepper flakes
1	red onion, chopped	2½	teaspoons Dijon mustard
¼	cup seasoned rice vinegar	2	tablespoons finely chopped fresh basil
1	(8-ounce) can crushed pineapple, with juice	¼	cup diced red bell pepper

In a skillet, heat the oil over medium heat. Add the garlic and onion and sauté about 2 minutes. Stir in the vinegar, pineapple with juice, allspice, red pepper flakes, and mustard. Heat, stirring, about 4 minutes or until bubbly and slightly thickened.

In a blender, puree the pineapple mixture until smooth; keep warm. Just before serving, stir in the basil and red bell pepper.

Makes 2 cups

Honey Jalapeño Chicken with Tomato Olivada

FAMILY CIRCLE/NATIONAL HONEY BOARD RECIPE CONTEST
Main Dish
Helen Conwell
Fairhope, Alabama

½ red jalapeño pepper, stemmed, seeded, and chopped

2 tablespoons honey

⅛ teaspoon salt, or to taste

4 boneless, skinless chicken breast halves (about 5 ounces each)

Tomato Olivada

2 tablespoons honey

1 medium tomato, peeled and cut in ½-inch cubes

¼ cup finely chopped green bell pepper

½ cup finely chopped red onion

12 Kalamata olives, pitted and coarsely chopped

1 tablespoon balsamic vinegar

1 tablespoon olive oil

⅛ teaspoon salt

Watercress sprigs, for garnish

Place the jalapeño, 2 tablespoons honey, and salt in a small blender or food processor. Whirl to puree. (Or blend the honey and salt with a mortar and pestle.) Rub the mixture over the chicken. Cover and refrigerate 1 hour.

Prepare an outdoor grill with medium-hot coals or preheat the broiler.

Grill the chicken, skin side down, or broil skin side up until browned, about 7 minutes. Turn the chicken over. Grill or broil until the chicken is no longer pink in the center, about 5 minutes.

Meanwhile, prepare the olivada: Mix together the honey, tomato, green pepper, red onion, olives, vinegar, oil, and salt in a small bowl. Serve the grilled chicken with the olivada. Garnish the plates with sprigs of fresh watercress.

Makes 4 servings

Greek-Style Chicken and Pasta

**FAST AND HEALTHY MAGAZINE/GREEN GIANT
RUSH-HOUR RECIPE CONTEST**
Grand Prize—$3,000
Julie DeMatteo
Clementon, New Jersey

Julie DeMatteo

Clementon, New Jersey

Julie states, "The thing I like most about contesting is the chance to be creative. I love seeing what I can do with a recipe to 'make it mine' and to feature the sponsor's product. Sometimes I think it takes more mental creativity and talent than it does culinary ability (although you must have that knowledge) to come up with something new, different, and designed to catch the judges' eyes and taste buds."

4 boneless, skinless chicken breast halves, cut into 2- x ½-inch strips

1 (1-pound) package Green Giant Pasta Accents Garden Herb Seasoning Frozen Vegetables and Pasta

1 (14½-ounce) can pasta-style chunky tomatoes, undrained

¼ cup sliced ripe olives

1 ounce feta cheese, crumbled (¼ cup)

Spray a large skillet with nonstick cooking spray. Heat over medium-high heat until the skillet is hot. Add the chicken; cook and stir until no longer pink. Add the frozen vegetables and pasta, tomatoes, and olives. Bring to a boil. Reduce the heat to low, cover, and simmer, stirring occasionally, 7 to 9 minutes or until the vegetables are crisp-tender and the chicken is fork-tender and no longer pink. Sprinkle with the cheese.

Makes 4 servings

Gingered Jamaican Jerk Chicken

41st National Chicken Cooking Contest
Second Place—$5,000
Diane Lentz
Nicholasville, Kentucky

1 tablespoon chili powder
1½ teaspoons curry powder
1½ teaspoons dried thyme
1 teaspoon paprika
1 teaspoon coarsely ground black pepper
½ teaspoon ground cumin
½ teaspoon granulated garlic
½ teaspoon salt
¼ teaspoon ground allspice
¼ teaspoon cayenne pepper

4 boneless, skinless chicken breast halves
3 tablespoons olive oil
⅓ cup finely diced fresh ginger
6 large slices red onion
2 tablespoons butter
3 tablespoons lemon juice
3 Granny Smith apples, peeled, cored, and thinly sliced
⅓ cup light brown sugar
Parsley sprigs, for garnish

In a small bowl, make the jerk seasoning by mixing together the chili powder, curry powder, thyme leaves, paprika, pepper, cumin, garlic, salt, allspice, and cayenne pepper. Sprinkle over the chicken, coating both sides.

In a large skillet, heat the oil over medium-high heat. Add the chicken and ginger; cook about 10 minutes or until a fork can be inserted in the chicken with ease. Remove the chicken from the skillet and keep warm. In the same skillet, cook the onion slices, turning once, about 3 minutes or until tender. Remove and set aside. Melt the butter in the skillet, then add the lemon juice and apples. Sauté the apples until they begin to soften. Add the brown sugar and cook until the liquid is reduced and thickens. Arrange the onion slices on a serving plate and top with the chicken, then the apple mixture. Garnish with parsley.

Makes 4 servings

Chicken Picante

1985 NATIONAL CHICKEN COOKING CONTEST
Runner-up
Sally Vog
Springfield, Oregon

Sally Vog
Springfield, Oregon

When Sally returned home from winning the National Chicken Cooking Contest, she was invited to appear in a television commercial. A recipe card with her picture on it was even available in the poultry section of supermarkets, and she received a two-year supply of free chicken for her family. Sally's tip to those new to cook-offs at which the media and public are able to watch and ask questions: Do not allow yourself to be distracted during the cooking time. Give your recipe your undivided attention.

½ cup medium chunky taco sauce
¼ cup Dijon mustard
2 tablespoons fresh lime juice
6 boneless, skinless chicken breast halves
2 tablespoons butter

6 tablespoons plain yogurt
1 lime, peeled, sliced into 6 segments, membrane removed
Chopped fresh cilantro, for garnish

In a large bowl, make a marinade by mixing the taco sauce, mustard, and lime juice. Add the chicken, turning to coat. Marinate for at least 30 minutes.

In a large skillet, melt the butter over medium heat until foamy. Remove the chicken from the marinade and place in the skillet. Cook, turning, about 10 minutes or until golden brown on all sides. Add the marinade and cook about 5 minutes more, until a fork can be inserted in the chicken with ease and the marinade is slightly re-duced and beginning to glaze. Remove the chicken to a warmed serving platter.

Raise the heat to high and boil the marinade 1 minute; pour over the chicken. Place 1 tablespoon of the yogurt on each breast half and top each with a lime segment. Garnish with chopped cilantro.

Makes 6 servings

Caribbean Chicken Drums

40TH NATIONAL CHICKEN COOKING CONTEST
Grand Prize
Rosemarie Berger
Jamestown, North Carolina

2 tablespoons oil

8 broiler-fryer chicken drumsticks

1 (14½-ounce) can whole peeled tomatoes, cut in chunks

1 (4-ounce) can diced green chilies

1 tablespoon brown sugar

¼ teaspoon ground allspice

¼ cup chopped mango chutney

1 tablespoon fresh lemon juice

¼ cup dark seedless raisins

1 large banana, sliced

1 ripe mango, sliced

In a skillet, heat the oil over medium heat. Add the chicken and cook, turning, about 10 minutes or until browned on all sides. Add the tomatoes, chilies, brown sugar, and allspice. Bring to a boil, cover, reduce the heat to low, and cook 20 minutes. Add the chutney, lemon juice, and raisins. Cover and cook about 15 minutes or until a fork can be inserted in the chicken with ease. Remove the chicken to a serving platter.

Skim off the fat from the sauce. Add the banana to the skillet; heat thoroughly. Spoon the banana and a little sauce over the chicken. Garnish with mango slices. Place the remaining sauce in a separate dish and serve.

Makes 4 servings

Caribbean Chicken Fajitas

40TH NATIONAL CHICKEN COOKING CONTEST
Third Place
Kim Landhuis
Fort Dodge, Iowa

4 boneless, skinless chicken breast halves, cut in long strips
1 teaspoon garlic salt
½ teaspoon seasoned pepper
½ tablespoon vegetable oil
2 large cloves garlic, minced
1 green bell pepper, roasted (see Note), cut in strips
1 gold bell pepper, roasted, cut in strips
1 red bell pepper, roasted, cut in strips
1 yellow bell pepper, roasted, cut in strips
⅓ cup julienned jicama
⅓ cup chopped scallions
⅓ cup sliced red onion
10 (6½-inch) flour tortillas
Orange Picante Salsa (recipe follows)

Place the chicken in a shallow bowl and sprinkle with the garlic salt and seasoned pepper. Stir to coat. Heat the oil in a skillet over medium-high heat. Add the garlic and sauté 1 minute. Add the chicken and cook, stirring, about 10 minutes or until fork-tender. Remove from the heat.

In a large bowl, mix together the peppers, jicama, scallions, and red onion. On a warm serving platter, arrange in three parts the chicken, pepper mixture, and tortillas and set out a bowl of Orange Picante Salsa. Fill each tortilla with some chicken, pepper mixture, and salsa and fold both sides over the filling.

Makes 5 servings

Note: To roast the peppers, place under the broiler and turn until charred. Let cool. With a knife point, remove the stem, seeds, and skin.

Orange Picante Salsa

1   cup bottled picante sauce
2   tablespoons orange marmalade
¼   cup chopped fresh cilantro

In a medium bowl, stir all the ingredients together.

Makes 1¼ cups

Extra-Crisp Cilantro-Crusted Fried Chicken

WESSON "WAIT TILL YOU TASTE MY FRIED CHICKEN" RECIPE CONTEST
Winner
Josephine Piro
Easton, Pennsylvania

Josephine Piro

Easton, Pennsylvania

Josephine's contesting tips are: make sure the recipes you enter are easy to prepare and have a good presentation; try to stay away from expensive items that average cooks couldn't afford to buy; do not use equipment the average cook may not have available; use the sponsor's product in a way that might not have occurred to them; and keep up with new products and current food trends.

---

1   fryer chicken (about 3 pounds), cut up
¾   cup all-purpose flour
¾   cup whole wheat flour
¼   teaspoon salt
¼   teaspoon black pepper
3   tablespoons chopped fresh cilantro, or 1 tablespoon dried

2   tablespoons grated Parmesan cheese
1   teaspoon paprika
¼   teaspoon ground ginger
¼   teaspoon ground allspice
¼   cup Wesson Canola Oil

Rinse the chicken well and pat dry. Sift the flours, salt, pepper, cilantro, cheese, paprika, ginger, and allspice into a paper or plastic bag to mix well. Drop the chicken pieces 2 or 3 at a time into the bag, hold the bag closed, and shake it until the chicken is thoroughly covered. Transfer the chicken to a wire rack and refrigerate it for 2 hours, or place the chicken pieces on a baking sheet and freeze briefly, about 5 minutes, to set the coating. Reserve the flour mixture.

Heat the oil in a large heavy skillet over medium-high heat. Dredge the chicken in the flour mixture to coat again, shaking off the excess. Discard the remaining flour mixture. When the oil is hot, add the chicken and brown 2 minutes on each side, making sure the pan is not crowded. Lower the heat and continue cooking 5 to 6 minutes longer on each side, until the chicken is firm to the touch and juices from the thigh run clear when pricked with a fork.

Transfer the chicken to a warmed platter and serve immediately.

Makes 4 servings

Chicken Breasts Diavolo

NEWMAN'S OWN/GOOD HOUSEKEEPING ANNUAL RECIPE CONTEST
Grand Prize

Geraldine Kirkpatrick
Huntington, California

6 large boneless, skinless chicken breast halves, slightly flattened

½ cup finely minced fresh parsley

1 teaspoon lemon pepper

Pinch salt

Pinch garlic powder

3 tablespoons olive oil

3 (6-ounce) jars marinated artichoke hearts

1 tablespoon fresh lemon juice

1 26-ounce jar Newman's Own Bandito Diavolo Sauce

½ cup red wine (Chianti preferred)

1½ cups shredded mozzarella cheese

1½ cups onion-garlic croutons tossed with 1 tablespoon olive oil

6 cups cooked pasta or rice

Preheat oven to 350 degrees.

Sprinkle the chicken with the parsley, lemon pepper, salt, and garlic powder. Roll up each breast, seasoned side in, and secure with a wooden toothpick. Sauté in the oil in a large skillet until golden brown. Remove from the pan and place in a 13x9-inch baking pan. Carefully remove the toothpicks.

Drain the artichoke hearts, sprinkle with the lemon juice, and distribute among the rolled chicken breasts. Combine the diavolo sauce with the wine and pour over the chicken and artichokes. Spread the shredded mozzarella evenly over the top. Sprinkle with croutons as a topping. Bake 30 to 40 minutes, until golden brown and bubbly.

While the chicken is baking, prepare the pasta or rice. Spoon the cooked chicken breasts over the pasta or rice and serve with crusty Italian bread or rolls, a green salad with olive oil and vinegar dressing, and the rest of the wine.

Makes 6 servings

Baked Chicken with Red-Peppered Onions

1990 Delmarva Chicken Cooking Contest

First Place

Ellen Burr

Truro, Massachusetts

1   broiler-fryer chicken, quartered
2   teaspoons lemon pepper
1   teaspoon olive oil
4   cups thinly sliced sweet onions

4   tablespoons red hot-pepper jelly
1   small red bell pepper, cut in rings, for garnish
Cilantro sprigs, for garnish

Preheat the oven to 400 degrees. Oil the rack in a large roasting pan.

Place the chicken on the rack and sprinkle with the lemon pepper. Bake skin side up for 50 minutes or until fork-tender.

Meanwhile, in a large nonstick skillet, heat the oil over medium heat. Add the onions and cook until barely wilted, about 5 minutes. Add the jelly and stir gently until melted. Spoon half of the onion mixture onto a large platter. Arrange the chicken over the onions; top with the remaining onions. Garnish with pepper rings and cilantro.

Makes 4 servings

Chicken with Mushrooms and Sage Cream

1996 DELMARVA CHICKEN COOKING CONTEST
First Place
Julie Fox
Annapolis, Maryland

4 boneless, skinless chicken breast halves

2 tablespoons flour

¼ teaspoon salt

⅛ teaspoon freshly ground black pepper

3 teaspoons olive oil

2 cloves garlic, minced

1½ cups sliced cremini or white button mushrooms

¾ cup chopped scallions

½ cup dry white wine

1 (8-ounce) package low-fat cream cheese, cubed

½ cup grated Parmesan cheese, plus additional for serving

¼ cup low-fat milk

2 tablespoons chopped fresh sage

4 cups hot cooked linguine

Fresh sage leaves, for garnish

On a hard surface, pound the chicken with a meat mallet or similar utensil to ¼-inch thickness. In a shallow dish, mix together the flour, salt, and pepper. Add the chicken, one piece at a time, turning to coat on all sides.

In a large nonstick skillet, heat the oil over medium-high heat. Add the chicken and cook, turning, about 8 minutes or until browned and fork-tender. Arrange the chicken on a platter; cover loosely, and keep warm.

To the drippings in the skillet, add the garlic, mushrooms, scallions, and wine. Cook, covered, over medium-low heat 3 minutes or until the vegetables are tender. Add the cream cheese, ½ cup Parmesan, milk, and chopped sage; stir constantly until the cheeses melt and the sauce is smooth.

Place the linguine on 4 serving plates and arrange the chicken on top. Spoon the mushrooms and sage cream over the chicken. Garnish with fresh sage leaves and serve with additional Parmesan.

Makes 4 servings

Note: If the sauce becomes too thick, add more low-fat milk or some fat-free chicken broth.

Parisian Walnut-Dijon Chicken

1992 PREMIUM YOUNG'N TENDER BRAND CHICKEN
WINNING TASTE RECIPE CONTEST
Grand Prize
Manika Misra
North Miami Beach, Florida

6 Young'n Tender Brand boneless, skinless chicken breast halves
2 tablespoons butter
1 clove garlic, minced
½ cup minced onion
2 ounces cream cheese
¾ cup finely chopped walnuts
½ teaspoon salt
¼ teaspoon black pepper
¼ cup Dijon mustard
½ cup half-and-half
½ cup seeded, chopped tomatoes
2 tablespoons chopped fresh parsley
1 cup sliced onions (optional)

Place the chicken breasts between sheets of plastic wrap or waxed paper and flatten with a meat mallet until ¼ inch thick. Melt 1 tablespoon of the butter in a small sauté pan. Add the garlic and minced onion; sauté until tender. Add the cream cheese, walnuts, salt, and pepper. Sauté about 1 minute, until blended. Divide the mixture and set half aside.

Preheat the broiler.

Place about 1 tablespoon of the walnut mixture on each breast; fold the chicken over the filling and place on a baking pan. Reserve 1 tablespoon of the mustard. Brush the remaining mustard on both sides of the chicken. Broil 4 to 6 inches from the heat source for 6 to 8 minutes per side or until done.

Prepare a sauce by combining the remaining half of the walnut mixture with the re-served tablespoon mustard, half-and-half, tomatoes, and parsley. Simmer over low heat until slightly thickened, 2 to 3 minutes.

If desired, melt the remaining tablespoon butter in a small skillet and sauté the sliced onions about 10 minutes or until golden. Place the chicken on a platter and top with the sauce and sautéed onions. Serve with rice or pasta.

Makes 6 servings

Southwestern Chicken Sandwiches

HELLMANN'S/BEST FOODS RECIPE CONTEST
Winner
Paula McHargue
Richmond, Kentucky

Sauce

- ½ cup Hellmann's or Best Foods mayonnaise (do not use low-fat)
- ¼ cup chopped sun-dried tomatoes packed in oil, drained
- ½ teaspoon ground cumin

Sandwiches

- ½ cup Hellmann's or Best Foods mayonnaise
- 1 tablespoon lime juice
- 1 teaspoon chili powder
- ½ teaspoon ground red pepper
- 4 boneless, skinless chicken breast halves (about 1 pound)
- 4 (6- to 7-inch) sandwich rolls, halved lengthwise
- 4 red leaf lettuce leaves
- 4 slices Monterey Jack or cheddar cheese

Preheat the broiler. In a small bowl, combine the ingredients for the sauce; set aside.

To make the sandwiches, in another small bowl, combine the mayonnaise, lime juice, chili powder, and ground red pepper. Place the chicken on the rack of a broiler pan and brush with half of the mayonnaise mixture. Place the pan 5 to 7 inches from the heat and broil the chicken 7 to 9 minutes. Turn; brush with the remaining mayonnaise mixture. Continue broiling 7 to 9 minutes or until the chicken is no longer pink in the center.

To serve, spread the sauce over the cut surfaces of each roll. Place a lettuce leaf on the bottom half of each roll. Layer with the chicken, cheese, and top of the roll.

Makes 4 servings

Turkey

Waikiki Turkey Sandwich

HELLMANN'S/BEST FOODS RECIPE CONTEST
First Place
Loanne Chiu
Fort Worth, Texas

Loanne Chiu

Fort Worth, Texas

Loanne, a psychologist, is of Chinese ancestry but was born in Indonesia, educated in Germany, and now lives in the United States. It was during her travels, especially a trip to China, that she became fascinated by the distinctly different cuisines of each region. She especially was struck by the attention paid to color and presentation of a dish. It is that attention to detail that catches the judges' imagination and makes Loanne a frequent winner.

1 cup Hellmann's or Best Foods mayonnaise (not low fat)	8 frozen ground turkey burgers, thawed
3 tablespoons finely chopped scallions	8 canned pineapple slices, drained
½ teaspoon pumpkin pie spice	4 Thomas' English Muffins or hamburger buns, split and toasted
½ teaspoon freshly ground black pepper	8 Boston lettuce leaves

Prepare an outdoor grill.

In a small bowl, combine ½ cup of the mayonnaise and the scallions; set aside.

In another bowl, stir the remaining ½ cup mayonnaise with the pumpkin pie spice and pepper. Spread evenly on both sides of the turkey burgers. Grill the burgers over high heat 8 to 10 minutes, just until browned and cooked through. Grill the pineapple slices.

Spread each muffin half with the scallion mayonnaise. Layer with lettuce, grilled turkey burgers, and pineapple slices.

Makes 4 servings

Quick Turkey Appetizers

1993 NATIONAL TURKEY LOVERS' TEEN RECIPE CONTEST
Grand Prize
Shiloh Graham
Acton, California

6 large (10-inch) flour tortillas	1 medium tomato, chopped
4 teaspoons olive oil	2 tablespoons chopped fresh cilantro
1 cup salsa	1½ tablespoons chopped black olives
1 pound sliced deli smoked turkey, cut into ¼-inch-thick strips	½ teaspoon crushed red pepper
	1 cup grated Monterey Jack cheese

Preheat the oven to 400 degrees.

Place the tortillas on two 12x14-inch baking sheets. Lightly brush both sides of the tortillas with the oil. Bake the tortillas 3 minutes; remove from the oven.

Evenly spread the salsa over each tortilla to within ½ inch of the edge. Sprinkle the turkey, tomato, cilantro, olives, red pepper, and Monterey Jack evenly over the salsa on each tortilla. Bake 10 to 12 minutes or until the cheese melts.

To serve, slice each tortilla in 8 wedges.

Makes 6 servings

Thai Turkey Toss

NATIONAL TURKEY LOVERS' RECIPE CONTEST
First Place
Judy Warren
North Carolina

1 pound turkey breast cutlets

1 cup lightly salted water

5 ounces rice vermicelli

3 cups boiling water

2 cups shredded fresh spinach

1½ cups diced Granny Smith apples

½ cup grated carrot

½ cup peeled and diced zucchini

⅓ cup coarsely chopped dry-roasted peanuts

2 tablespoons chopped fresh basil

Thai Dressing (recipe follows)

In a large skillet, arrange the turkey in a single layer. Add the lightly salted water and bring to a boil. Cover, reduce the heat, and simmer 5 to 10 minutes or until no longer pink inside. Allow the turkey to cool and cut into 1½x¼-inch strips.

Break the vermicelli into 3-inch pieces and place in a heatproof bowl. Add the boiling water and allow the pasta to stand 6 to 8 minutes or until soft; drain well.

In a large bowl, combine the turkey, vermicelli, spinach, apples, carrot, zucchini, peanuts, and basil. To serve, toss with the dressing and divide evenly among 4 plates.

Makes 4 servings

Thai Dressing

¼ cup fish sauce (soy sauce may be substituted)

3 tablespoons fresh lime juice

2 tablespoons brown sugar

1½ teaspoons minced fresh ginger

1 large clove garlic, minced

¼ teaspoon crushed red pepper

In a small bowl, combine all the ingredients.

Makes scant ⅔ cup

Chili Turkey 'n' Sweet Potato Stew with Corn Bread Dumplings

TOPSY-TURVY TURKEY RECIPE CONTEST
Second Prize—Adult
Julie DeMatteo
Clementon, *New Jersey*

Corn Bread Dumplings

1   (6½-ounce) package corn muffin mix
1   teaspoon ground cumin
1   egg
2   tablespoons margarine or butter, melted
3   to 5 tablespoons milk

Stew

¼   cup all-purpose flour
½   teaspoon ground cumin
1½ pounds turkey thighs, skinned, boned, and cut in 1-inch cubes
4   teaspoons vegetable oil
1   medium onion, chopped
2   cloves garlic, minced
1   medium sweet potato, peeled and cubed
4   cups chicken broth
1½ cups picante sauce
1   teaspoon dried oregano
1   medium zucchini, unpeeled, cut into ½-inch cubes
1   (15-ounce) can black beans, rinsed and drained
1   cup frozen corn kernels
1   (4-ounce) can chopped mild green chilies, drained

To make the dumplings: In a large bowl, combine the muffin mix, cumin, egg, and margarine. Add milk until the batter is thick.

To make the stew: In a medium bowl, combine the flour, cumin, and turkey cubes. Lightly toss until the cubes are coated; shake off the excess flour mixture.

In a large skillet over medium-high heat, cook the turkey in 2 teaspoons of the oil 5 to 6 minutes, until all sides are browned. Remove to a bowl.

In the same skillet, sauté the onion, garlic, and sweet potato in the remaining 2 teaspoons of oil 3 to 5 minutes, until the onion is softened. Add the turkey to the mixture and stir in the broth, picante sauce, and oregano. Cover and simmer 10 to 12 minutes, until heated throughout. Add the zucchini, black beans, corn, and chilies; bring to a boil.

Spoon the dumpling batter on top of the stew by teaspoonfuls. Reduce the heat and simmer, covered, 10 to 12 minutes. Remove the cover and simmer 5 to 7 minutes or until the dumplings are cooked through and the turkey and vegetables are tender.

Makes 4 servings

Garlic-Crusted Tuscany Burgers

1994 KRETSCHMER WHEAT GERM
"HEALTHY EATING MADE EASY & DELICIOUS" RECIPE CONTEST
First Prize—Main Dish

Kurt Wait

Redwood City, California

Sun-Dried Tomato Topping

⅓ cup sun-dried tomatoes

⅓ cup plain nonfat or low-fat yogurt

2 tablespoons chopped fresh basil, or 1½ teaspoons dried

Burgers

1 pound ground turkey breast

½ cup Kretschmer original toasted wheat germ

½ cup finely chopped onion

2 tablespoons water

1 teaspoon dried oregano

½ teaspoon dried fennel leaves, crushed

½ teaspoon salt (optional)

½ teaspoon black pepper

⅛ teaspoon ground allspice

2 teaspoons minced garlic

6 whole wheat hamburger buns, split and lightly toasted

6 lettuce leaves

To make the topping: Soften the tomatoes in boiling water, drain, and chop. Combine the tomatoes, yogurt, and basil; mix well. Set aside. (The topping may be made 1 day ahead and refrigerated until ready to use.)

Prepare an outdoor grill or preheat the broiler.

To make the burgers: Combine all the burger ingredients except the garlic, lettuce, and buns; mix lightly but thoroughly. Shape the turkey mixture into six ½-inch-thick patties. Sprinkle the garlic evenly over both sides of the patties and press gently.

Place the patties on a rack over medium coals or on the rack of a broiler pan. Grill or broil 4 to 5 inches from the heat source 3 to 4 minutes per side or until no longer pink and the juices run clear.

Line the bottom half of each hamburger bun with lettuce; place a burger on top. Spread about 1 tablespoon topping on the burger and place the top half of the bun on top.

Makes 6 servings

Pecan-Stuffed Turkey Breast with Asparagus

BUTTERBALL SLICE'N SERVE MEAL MAKERS RECIPE CONTEST—1991

First Place

Joyce Campagna
Summerville, South Carolina

1 (1-pound) piece Butterball Slice'N Serve breast of turkey

½ cup water

3 tablespoons unsalted butter or margarine

1 cup crumbled dry stuffing mix

4 tablespoons chopped pecans

1 teaspoon onion powder

½ teaspoon paprika

1 cup sliced mushrooms

1 cup fresh asparagus pieces

1 tablespoon cornstarch

1 cup half-and-half

1 large egg yolk, beaten

½ cup sliced scallions

1 tablespoon dry sherry

½ teaspoon salt

Preheat the oven to 350 degrees.

Cut the turkey into 4 thick slices, about ¾ inch thick. Cut a pocket in the side of each slice.

Put the water and 1 tablespoon of the butter in a small saucepan. Bring to a boil over medium heat. Stir in the stuffing mix and 2 tablespoons of the pecans. Fill the pockets with the stuffing, packing it firmly but not tightly. Sprinkle the turkey slices with onion powder and paprika. Put the stuffed slices in an 8-inch square baking dish.

Melt the remaining 2 tablespoons butter in a large saucepan over medium heat. Add the mushrooms and asparagus pieces and cook, stirring, for about 4 minutes or until the asparagus is crisp-tender. Combine the cornstarch and half-and-half and stir until smooth. Add the mixture to the vegetables and cook until thickened. Gradually stir ½ cup of the half-and-half mixture into the egg yolk. Add the yolk mixture to the pan and cook until bubbling. Stir in the scallions, sherry, salt, and remaining 2 tablespoons pecans.

Spoon the asparagus mixture over the stuffed turkey slices and bake for 20 to 25 minutes or until hot.

Makes 4 servings

Lemon Turkey Stir-Fry with Pasta

1992 NATIONAL TURKEY LOVERS' RECIPE CONTEST
First Place
Matt McHargue
Richmond, Kentucky

1½ pounds turkey cutlets or slices, cut in ½-inch-wide strips

1 tablespoon soy sauce

1 tablespoon white wine vinegar

2 teaspoons cornstarch

1 teaspoon lemon pepper

2 tablespoons olive oil

6 scallions, sliced

1 lemon, cut in 10 thin slices and finely slivered

1 clove garlic, finely minced

1 (10-ounce) bag fresh spinach, washed, drained, and chopped

1 pound linguine, cooked according to package directions and drained

Parsley sprigs and lemon slices, for garnish (optional)

In a self-closing plastic bag, combine the turkey, soy sauce, vinegar, cornstarch, and lemon pepper. Shake the bag to coat the turkey thoroughly. Refrigerate 30 minutes to allow the flavors to blend.

In a large skillet over medium heat, sauté the turkey and marinade in the oil 2 to 3 minutes or until the turkey is no longer pink. Add the scallions, lemon slivers, and garlic; continue to cook until the scallions are translucent. Stir in the spinach and cook just until wilted.

To serve, toss the turkey mixture with the hot linguine and garnish with the parsley and lemon slices, if desired.

Makes 6 servings

Beef

Pacific Rim Glazed Flank Steak

1997 NATIONAL BEEF COOK-OFF
Grand Prize
Chris Freymuller
Salt Lake City, Utah

Chris Freymuller
Salt Lake City, Utah

Chris, an investment broker, earned a quick $25,000 in the National Beef Cook-Off with Pacific Rim Glazed Flank Steak, a recipe he frequently serves to guests. Although grilling is the method of preparation, Chris says he has loved all forms of cooking since childhood. He does not use food processors, choosing instead to chop his ingredients by hand. He also avoids prepackaged items, preferring to cook from scratch. Speaking from experience, this one is worth trying.

Marinade

1 cup prepared teriyaki marinade
½ cup chopped onion
⅓ cup honey
⅓ cup fresh orange juice
1 tablespoon chopped fresh rosemary
1 tablespoon toasted sesame oil
1 large clove garlic, crushed
Black pepper (optional)

1 beef flank steak (1½ to 2 pounds)
Orange slices and rosemary sprigs, for garnish

In a shallow dish, combine the marinade ingredients, adding pepper, if desired; whisk until blended. Remove and reserve ¾ cup for basting.

With a sharp knife, lightly score both sides of the flank steak in a crisscross pattern. Place the steak in the remaining marinade in the dish, turning to coat. Cover and marinate in the refrigerator for 30 minutes, turning once.

Meanwhile, prepare an outdoor grill.

Remove the steak from the marinade; discard marinade. Place the steak on the grill rack over medium, ash-covered coals. Grill, uncovered, 17 to 21 minutes for medium-rare to medium doneness, basting occasionally with reserved ¾ cup marinade and turning once.

Place the remaining basting marinade in a small saucepan; place on the grill rack and bring to a boil. Meanwhile, carve the steak diagonally across the grain into thin slices; arrange on a platter. Spoon the hot marinade over the beef, as desired. Garnish with orange slices and rosemary sprigs.

Makes 4 to 6 servings

Easy and Elegant Beef Stroganoff

WOMAN'S DAY/FRANCO-AMERICAN GRAVY CONTEST
Grand Prize
Ellen Burr
Truro, Massachusetts

Ellen Burr

Truro, Massachusetts

Ellen graduated magna cum laude from Radcliffe and received her master's from Boston University. It was through her studies in graduate school that she discovered her love for cooking by reading Elizabethan recipe books. The same elegance found in her reading is evident in her recipes. Over the years Ellen has won and placed in a wide variety of contests, but the theme that runs through them all is a keen knowledge of which ingredients work best together.

1 pound well-trimmed beef sirloin steak, cut across the grain in thin, bite-size strips

½ teaspoon pepper, preferably white

2 tablespoons butter or margarine

6 ounces portobello or large white mushrooms, halved and thinly sliced (about 4 cups)

6 scallions, white part cut in ½-inch pieces, green part thinly sliced

1 (10½-ounce) can Franco-American Beef Gravy

2 tablespoons balsamic vinegar, or 1 tablespoon red wine vinegar

⅓ cup reduced-fat sour cream

Sprinkle the steak strips with half of the pepper.

Melt 1 tablespoon of the butter in a large, preferably nonstick skillet over medium-high heat. Add the mushrooms, white part of the scallions, and remaining pepper.

Cook, stirring often, until the mushrooms are tender, about 8 minutes. Remove with a slotted spoon to a bowl.

Wipe the skillet clean. Add the remaining butter and heat over high heat until sizzling. Add the beef strips and stir-fry about 2 minutes, until browned. Stir in the gravy and vinegar; bring to a boil. Remove from the heat and stir in the sour cream until blended. Sprinkle with the green part of the scallions. Serve immediately.

Makes 6 servings

Grecian Skillet Rib-Eyes

NATIONAL BEEF COOK-OFF
Grand Prize—Best of Beef
Fran Yuhas
Scotrun, Pennsylvania

Seasonings

1½ teaspoons garlic powder

1½ teaspoons dried basil, crushed

1½ teaspoons dried oregano, crushed

½ teaspoon salt

⅛ teaspoon black pepper

2 well-trimmed beef rib-eye steaks, cut 1 inch thick (about 1 pound)

1 tablespoon olive oil

1 tablespoon fresh lemon juice

2 tablespoons crumbled feta cheese

1 tablespoon chopped pitted Kalamata or ripe olives

Lemon slices (optional)

Combine the seasoning ingredients; press into both sides of the beef steaks.

In a large nonstick skillet, heat the oil over medium heat until hot. Place the steaks in the skillet and cook 10 to 14 minutes for medium-rare to medium doneness, turning once. Sprinkle with the lemon juice.

To serve, sprinkle the cheese and olives over the steaks; garnish with lemon slices, if desired.

Makes 2 to 4 servings

Tip: Recipe may be doubled.

Santa Fe-Shanghai Beef

MARVELOUS MARINADE RECIPE CONTEST
Third Place
Lisa Keys
Middlebury, Connecticut

Lisa Keys

Middlebury, Connecticut

Lisa leads such an active life that it's a wonder she has time to cook. Outside her job as a physician's assistant, she plays softball and tennis. She and husband, William, have a son and daughter. As it happens, William is also a physician's assistant. Lisa has helped to compile several cookbooks. Reading so many recipes must be the source of her success, since Lisa's name shows up regularly on winners' lists.

Marinade

¼ cup olive oil

3 tablespoons fresh lime juice

1 tablespoon chopped fresh cilantro

2 cloves garlic, minced

2 teaspoons ground cumin

¼ teaspoon black pepper

Gallon-size Ziploc storage bag

1 pound trimmed boneless beef sirloin steak, cut 1 inch thick

2 tablespoons olive oil

1 cup thinly sliced green bell pepper

4 ounces fresh snow peas, trimmed

½ (7-ounce) jar baby corn, drained

⅓ cup sliced scallions

¼ cup red pepper jelly

¼ teaspoon salt

Chopped fresh cilantro, for garnish (optional)

Combine all the marinade ingredients in a gallon-size Ziploc storage bag. Seal the bag and shake to blend. Place the steak in the bag; remove excess air, reseal the bag, and turn to coat. Refrigerate 4 hours or overnight, turning once.

Prepare an outdoor grill.

Remove the steak from the bag, reserving the marinade. Grill the steak over medium-hot coals 5 minutes per side for medium-rare, or to desired doneness. Let the steak cool on a carving board 10 minutes.

Heat the oil in a skillet. Add the bell pepper and snow peas; stir-fry 2 minutes. Add the corn and scallions; stir-fry 1 minute. Remove the vegetables from the skillet. Add the reserved marinade and pepper jelly to the skillet. Boil the mixture, stirring constantly, 5 minutes or until the sauce thickens slightly; remove from the heat.

Thinly slice the steak crosswise; season with salt. Arrange the steak and vegetables on a platter; spoon the sauce over the meat and vegetables. Garnish with cilantro, if desired.

Makes 4 servings

Venezuelan Mystery Pie

Betty Crocker Create-a-Casserole Recipe Contest
Grand Prize
Linda Morten
Katy, Texas

Linda Morten

Katy, Texas

Linda, who was born in Venezuela, has traveled extensively and even attended high school in Singapore. A competitive roller skater, she especially enjoys ballroom dancing on skates. Linda also likes to use strong, powerful spices and unusual combinations of ingredients and flavors. She enjoys "smuggling" nutritious foods into the meals she makes for her husband and three daughters. It must be working, at least on the girls, because they have all been recognized in contests for their culinary ability.

½ cup yellow cornmeal

2½ cups chicken broth

½ teaspoon garlic salt

¼ cup (½ stick) margarine or butter

1 egg, beaten

¼ cup (1 ounce) shredded Colby cheese

1 pound ground beef, pork, sausage, or turkey

1 small green bell pepper, chopped (about ½ cup)

1 medium onion, chopped (about ½ cup)

⅓ cup sliced pimiento-stuffed olives

1 cup hot thick and chunky salsa

1 cup sour cream

1 cup (4 ounces) shredded sharp cheddar cheese

⅓ cup mayonnaise or salad dressing

Paprika, bell pepper slices, and scallion curls, for garnish (optional)

Preheat the oven to 375 degrees. Grease a 10-inch pie plate.

Heat the cornmeal, broth, and garlic salt to boiling in a large saucepan, stirring constantly; remove from the heat. Stir in the margarine and egg; fold in the Colby. Spread the cornmeal mixture on the bottom and up the sides of the pie plate. Flute the edge using oiled fingers.

Cook the ground meat in a medium skillet, stirring frequently, until browned; drain. Stir in the bell pepper, onion, and olives. Cook 5 minutes, stirring constantly, until the vegetables are crisp-tender. Stir in the salsa; simmer, uncovered, 5 minutes. Spoon the mixture into the pie plate. Cover with aluminum foil; bake 25 to 30 minutes or until hot.

Mix the sour cream, cheddar, and mayonnaise together; spread over the meat mixture. Bake, uncovered, 15 minutes more. Let stand 15 minutes before serving. Garnish with paprika, bell pepper slices, and scallion curls, if desired.

Makes 8 servings

Pronto Spicy Beef and Black Bean Salsa

1993 NATIONAL BEEF COOK-OFF
Grand Prize—$20,000
Sylvia Harber
Boulder City, Nevada

Seasoning

1 tablespoon chili powder

1 teaspoon ground cumin

1 teaspoon salt

½ teaspoon ground red pepper (cayenne)

1 beef tri-tip (bottom sirloin) roast or top sirloin steak, cut 1½ inches thick, trimmed of fat

1 (15-ounce) can black beans, rinsed and drained

1 medium tomato, chopped

1 small red onion, finely chopped

3 tablespoons coarsely chopped fresh cilantro

Fresh cilantro sprigs, for garnish (optional)

Prepare an outdoor grill.

Combine the seasoning ingredients; reserve 2 teaspoons for the salsa. Press the remaining seasoning mixture evenly onto the surface of the roast.

Grill the tri-tip over medium coals (medium-low coals for top sirloin) for 30 to 35 minutes (top sirloin 22 to 30 minutes) for rare to medium doneness, turning occasionally. Let stand 10 minutes before carving.

Meanwhile, in a medium bowl, combine beans, tomato, onion, chopped cilantro, and reserved seasoning mixture; stir until blended.

Carve the roast across the grain into slices. Arrange the beef and the bean salsa on a serving platter; garnish with cilantro sprigs, if desired.

Makes 6 servings

Oriental Short Rib Barbecue

1988 NATIONAL BEEF COOK-OFF
First Place
John Michels
Minnesota

⅔ cup thinly sliced scallions

½ cup soy sauce

½ cup water

¼ cup toasted sesame oil

2½ tablespoons packed brown sugar

1½ tablespoons sesame seeds, toasted and crushed

1 tablespoon minced garlic

1 tablespoon grated fresh ginger

½ teaspoon ground red pepper (cayenne)

⅛ teaspoon freshly ground Szechuan peppercorns

4 pounds beef short ribs, trimmed of excess fat and cut crosswise no more than ⅜ to ½ inch thick

Fresh red chili peppers, scallions, and radish roses, for garnish

Combine the scallions, soy sauce, water, sesame oil, brown sugar, sesame seeds, garlic, ginger, red pepper, and Szechuan peppercorns. Place this mixture and the short ribs in a plastic bag or utility dish and turn the ribs to coat. Close the bag securely or cover the dish and marinate in the refrigerator 4 to 6 hours, turning occasionally.

Prepare an outdoor grill.

Remove the ribs from the marinade, reserving the marinade. Grill the ribs over medium coals 5 to 6 minutes. Turn the ribs over and brush or spoon on the marinade. Cover and continue cooking 5 to 6 minutes or until the desired degree of doneness. Place the ribs on a platter; garnish with chili peppers, scallions, and radish roses.

Makes 6 servings

Peppered Sesame Beef Strips with Artichoke Hearts

1991 SOUTH CAROLINA BEEF COOK-OFF

First Place

Katherine Moss

Gaffney, South Carolina

4 beef sirloin strips (4 to 6 ounces), cut ½ inch thick

1 tablespoon peppercorns, crushed

¼ teaspoon garlic powder

¼ teaspoon ground ginger

2 tablespoons toasted sesame oil

¼ teaspoon lemon juice

¼ teaspoon grated lemon zest

1 tablespoon low-sodium soy sauce

3 tablespoons cooking sherry

1 (14-ounce) can artichoke hearts, drained

1 tablespoon sesame seeds, toasted

Lemon slices, for garnish

Trim any fat from the beef. Sprinkle the pepper, garlic powder, and ginger on each side of the steaks. Heat the sesame oil in a skillet over medium-high heat. Add the meat and cook about 2 minutes on each side or until medium doneness. Remove to a platter. Wipe out the skillet with paper towels.

Add the lemon juice, lemon zest, soy sauce, sherry, and artichoke hearts to the skillet and cook over low heat until thoroughly heated, stirring constantly. Place the artichokes on the beef platter. Spoon the pan juices over the warm beef strips. Sprinkle with toasted sesame seeds. Garnish with lemon slices.

Makes 4 servings

Spanish Steak Roll with Sautéed Vegetables

1991 NATIONAL BEEF COOK-OFF

Best of Beef

Sandy Collins

West Ridge, Colorado

1 pound trimmed boneless beef top sirloin steak, cut ¾ inch thick

1 teaspoon garlic powder

¼ teaspoon freshly ground black pepper

2 teaspoons vegetable oil

1 teaspoon butter

¾ teaspoon salt

1 medium red bell pepper, cut lengthwise into strips (about 3 cups)

1 medium green bell pepper, cut lengthwise into strips (about 3 cups)

1 small white onion, thinly sliced

1 cup sliced fresh mushrooms

⅓ cup chopped walnuts

¼ teaspoon chili powder

1 tablespoon sour cream

2 tablespoons drained chopped canned green chilies

Lemon slices and cilantro sprigs, for garnish

Pound the steak with the flat side of a meat mallet to about ¼-inch thickness. Combine ½ teaspoon of the garlic powder with the pepper; sprinkle over the steak. Heat 1 teaspoon of the oil and the butter in a large heavy skillet over medium-high heat until hot. Pan-fry the steak 5 to 7 minutes for medium-rare or to desired doneness, turning once. Remove the steak to a heated platter; sprinkle with ½ teaspoon of the salt. Keep warm.

Add the remaining 1 teaspoon oil to the skillet. Add the red and green peppers, onion, mushrooms, and walnuts. Cook 2 minutes, stirring frequently. Combine the remaining ½ teaspoon garlic powder, ¼ teaspoon salt, and chili powder; sprinkle over the vegetables and continue cooking 2 minutes, stirring frequently.

Spread the steak with the sour cream; top with the chilies. Starting at a short side, roll up the steak, jelly roll fashion; secure with 4 wooden picks. Spoon the vegetables around the steak roll; garnish with lemon slices and cilantro sprigs.

To serve, carve the steak roll between the wooden picks; remove and discard the picks.

Makes 4 servings

Beef Tenderloin Mexicana

WORLD BEEF COOK-OFF
First Place—$2,000
Linda Morten
Katy, Texas

4 (5-ounce) beef tenderloin steaks
2 tablespoons fresh lime juice
2 tablespoons chili powder
2 tablespoons vegetable oil
2 teaspoons minced garlic
¼ teaspoon ground cumin
¼ teaspoon crushed red pepper

Creamy Cilantro Sauce

1 (4-ounce) can mild, medium, or hot chopped green chilies, undrained
½ cup heavy cream
½ cup sour cream
1 tablespoon chopped fresh cilantro

Garnish

Cilantro sprigs and red bell pepper rings or julienne cut red bell pepper strips

Place the steaks in a wide, shallow dish. Combine the lime juice, chili powder, 1 tablespoon of the oil, the garlic, cumin, and red pepper in a small bowl. Pour over the steaks and rub to coat.

Heat the remaining tablespoon of oil in a large, heavy nonstick skillet over medium-high heat. Cook the steaks 4 minutes on each side for medium-rare doneness. Transfer to a serving platter and keep warm.

To make the sauce: Place the green chilies in a blender and puree until smooth. Combine the chilies and heavy cream in a small saucepan. Bring to a gentle boil. Stir in the sour cream and cilantro. Cook until just heated through. Spoon the sauce over the steaks. Garnish with cilantro sprigs and red bell pepper rings or strips.

Makes 4 servings

Garden Dinner Casserole

BORDEN'S VIVA LIGHT BUTTER HEALTHY REDO RECIPE CONTEST
Main Dish Winner
Maya Kline
Boise, Idaho

2 pounds zucchini, sliced

½ cup diagonally sliced celery

2 cups shredded carrots

1 onion, chopped

1 cup reduced-fat sour cream

1 can condensed low-sodium cream of chicken soup (see Note)

½ teaspoon dried dill

8 ounces reduced-fat smoked sausage, thinly sliced

1 (6-ounce) package stuffing mix

½ cup Viva Light Butter, melted

Preheat the oven to 350 degrees. Oil a 3-quart casserole.

In a large saucepan, cook the zucchini, celery, carrots, and onion in boiling water 5 to 6 minutes, until crisp-tender; drain. Stir in the sour cream, soup, dill, and sausage.

In a medium bowl, combine the stuffing mix and melted butter; stir to mix. Spread half of the mixture in the bottom of the prepared casserole. Pour the vegetable mixture over the stuffing; sprinkle the remaining stuffing over the vegetables. Bake 30 to 40 minutes or until golden brown.

Makes 6 servings

Note: You may use any cream soup; cream of broccoli or corn or cheddar soup will work very well.

Mexican Crock-Pot Meatloaf

THE GREAT AMERICAN MEATLOAF NATIONAL RECIPE CONTEST
First Place—Meatloaf with a Kick Category
Nancy Crew
Napoleon, Ohio

2 pounds ground beef

⅔ cup taco sauce

4 tablespoons packaged taco mix (add more if you'd like a spicier loaf)

2 cups coarsely crushed corn chips (more if needed)

2 large eggs, lightly beaten

1 cup grated Monterey Jack or cheddar cheese

In a large bowl, mix all the ingredients. Shape into a loaf and place in a Crock-Pot. Cover and cook on low 8 to 10 hours or on high 3½ to 5 hours.

Makes 8 servings

Veal & Lamb

Citrus-Rubbed Veal Chops with Sunshine Salsa

DISCOVER THE SPECIAL CHOICE OF VEAL RECIPE CONTEST
Best Grilled Veal Chop
Helen Conwell
Fairhope, Alabama

½ teaspoon salt

½ teaspoon grated lime zest

6 well-trimmed veal loin or rib chops, cut 1 inch thick (about 8 ounces each)

Sunshine Salsa (recipe follows)

Mint sprigs, for garnish

Prepare an outdoor grill.

In a small bowl, combine the salt and lime zest. Rub into both sides of the veal chops. Grill the chops over medium, ash-covered coals, 12 to 14 minutes, to medium doneness, turning occasionally. Serve with the salsa. Garnish with mint sprigs.

Makes 6 servings

Sunshine Salsa

1 mango, peeled, pitted, and cut into ½-inch cubes

½ cup salsa

¼ cup minced red onion

2 tablespoons fresh lime juice

In a medium bowl, combine the ingredients. Cover and refrigerate until serving time.

Makes about 2 cups

Mediterranean Veal Burgers

1996 Discover the Special Choice of Veal Recipe Contest
Best Grilled Ground Veal Recipe
Julie DeMatteo
Clementon, New Jersey

1 loaf (8 ounces) focaccia bread, about 8 inches in diameter

1 pound ground veal

1 egg

½ teaspoon salt

½ teaspoon black pepper

4 slices (¼ inch thick) unpeeled eggplant

⅓ cup plus 2 tablespoons prepared basil pesto

½ cup jarred roasted red peppers, rinsed, drained, and cut into strips

Prepare an outdoor grill.

Cut the focaccia into quarters. Using a serrated knife, split each quarter horizontally in half. Pull out ¼ inch soft bread from the cut side of the top of the focaccia; process in a food processor to make crumbs. Measure out ¼ cup crumbs for the veal mixture; reserve the remaining crumbs for another use (may be frozen up to 3 months).

In a medium bowl, combine the veal, bread crumbs, egg, salt, and pepper, mixing lightly but thoroughly. Shape into four ½-inch-thick patties.

Brush both sides of the eggplant slices with 2 tablespoons of the pesto. Place the veal patties in the center of the grill rack over medium, ash-covered coals. Place the eggplant slices around the edges of the rack. Grill 12 to 14 minutes or until the center of the burger is no longer pink and the eggplant slices are tender, turning once.

Place the focaccia, cut sides down, on the rack. Grill 1 to 2 minutes. Spread the remaining ⅓ cup pesto over the cut sides of the focaccia. Arrange the eggplant slices and red peppers on the bottoms of the focaccia; top with the burgers. Close the sandwiches.

Makes 4 servings

Grilled Veal Chops with Fresh Fruit Salsa

1994 FAVORITE VEAL RECIPE CONTEST
Grand Prize
Gloria Bradley
Naperville, Illinois

6   well-trimmed veal loin chops, cut 1
    inch thick
1   tablespoon olive oil

Salt and freshly ground white pepper
2   tablespoons chopped fresh cilantro
Fruit Salsa (recipe follows)

Prepare an outdoor grill.

Lightly brush the veal chops with the oil; season with salt and white pepper. Sprinkle cilantro on both sides of chops.

Grill the chops over medium coals 12 to 14 minutes, uncovered (10 to 12 minutes covered), for medium or to desired doneness, turning once. Serve with the salsa.

Makes 6 servings

Fruit Salsa

1   small ripe papaya, peeled, seeded,
    cut into ½-inch pieces
1   ripe nectarine, pitted and chopped
2   tablespoons finely chopped red bell
    pepper

1   jalapeño pepper, seeded and finely
    chopped
2   tablespoons chopped fresh cilantro
1   small scallion, thinly sliced
1   tablespoon olive oil

In a medium bowl, combine the ingredients; mix well. Cover and set aside until ready to use.

Makes 2 to 2½ cups

Veal Saté with Peanut Sauce

1995 Favorite Veal Recipe Contest

Jasmine Shane
Bayside, New York

1½ pounds veal leg cutlets, cut ⅛ to ¼ inch thick

Marinade

⅓ cup soy sauce

¼ cup fresh lime juice

2 tablespoons canned unsweetened coconut milk

1 tablespoon packed brown sugar

1 teaspoon freshly ground black pepper

Peanut Sauce

⅔ cup canned unsweetened coconut milk

¼ cup creamy peanut butter

½ to 1 teaspoon crushed red pepper

2 teaspoons grated lime zest

Cut the veal cutlets crosswise into 1-inch-wide strips. Combine the marinade ingredients; mix well. Place the veal and marinade in a plastic bag, turning to coat. Close the bag securely and marinate in the refrigerator 15 minutes to 1 hour, turning once.

Meanwhile, prepare an outdoor grill. Soak twelve 8-inch-long bamboo skewers in enough water to cover for 10 minutes; drain.

In a small bowl, whisk together the peanut sauce ingredients until blended; set aside. (If too thick, thin the sauce with 2 to 3 tablespoons water.)

Remove the veal from the marinade, discarding the marinade. Thread the veal, weaving back and forth, onto each skewer. Grill the veal over medium, ash-covered coals 4 to 5 minutes for medium doneness, turning once. Sprinkle with the lime peel. Serve with the sauce.

Makes 6 servings

Lamb Shanks Inferno

NEWMAN'S OWN/GOOD HOUSEKEEPING ANNUAL RECIPE CONTEST
Grand Prize
Sue Bloom
Dallas, Texas

4   lamb shanks
Salt and black pepper
¼   cup all-purpose flour
6   tablespoons olive oil
1   small onion, diced
2   cloves garlic, minced
1   carrot, diced

¾   cup dry red wine
¾   cup beef broth
1   (26-ounce) jar Newman's Own
    Diavolo Spicy Simmer Sauce or
    Newman's Own Bombolina Sauce
Parsley sprigs, for garnish

Preheat the oven to 350 degrees.

Season the lamb shanks with salt and pepper. Dredge in the flour, tapping off the excess.

Heat 5 tablespoons of the oil in a 5-quart Dutch oven until medium-hot. Brown 2 lamb shanks on all sides and remove from the Dutch oven. Repeat with the remaining 2 lamb shanks. Scrape out any accumulated browned bits from the bottom of the pan. Heat the remaining 1 tablespoon of oil until medium-hot. Sauté the onion and garlic until softened and translucent. Add the carrots; sauté an additional 1 to 2 minutes.

Add the wine to the vegetables. Increase the heat and reduce the wine by half. Add the broth and Newman's Own Diavolo Spicy Simmer Sauce. Heat the sauce just to boiling and immediately remove from the stove. Return the lamb shanks to the

Dutch oven. Spoon the sauce over the shanks, cover tightly, and place in the oven. Bake for 2 hours or until the meat is fork-tender.

Remove the shanks; keep warm. Skim the fat from the sauce. Adjust the seasonings and serve the sauce with the lamb shanks. Garnish with parsley sprigs. Serve with mashed potatoes, egg noodles, or rice.

Makes 4 servings

Pork

Orzo-Stuffed Tenderloin with Herbed Crust

JOHNSON & WALES UNIVERSITY NATIONAL HIGH SCHOOL RECIPE CONTEST
Grand Prize—Healthy Dinner Category
Wayne King
Montauk, New York

1¼ pounds lean pork tenderloin, trimmed

2 cups Orzo Stuffing (recipe follows)

¼ cup minced fresh rosemary

¼ cup minced fresh thyme

Freshly ground black pepper

¾ cup canned low-sodium chicken broth

½ teaspoon cornstarch dissolved in 2 tablespoons water

Preheat the oven to 350 degrees. Spray a roasting pan with vegetable oil cooking spray.

Make a horizontal cut in the pork tenderloin to create a pocket. Open the tenderloin like a book and place between 2 sheets of waxed paper. Flatten with a mallet until meat is of even thickness. Place the orzo stuffing lengthwise along the center of the tenderloin. Roll the meat up lengthwise, leaving the seam on the bottom. Tie the meat with butcher's string so it remains closed. Do not tie too tightly.

Roll the tenderloin in the minced herbs. Season with pepper. Sear the meat in a nonstick or cast-iron skillet until slightly browned. Transfer the meat to the prepared roasting pan and roast until the internal temperature reaches 160 degrees, about 30 minutes. Remove the meat from the pan. Let rest.

Deglaze the pan drippings with the broth. Strain the liquid into a small saucepan. Add the dissolved cornstarch and stir over medium heat until slightly thickened.

Untie the string on the tenderloin. Cut the meat into 8 slices, providing 2 slices per serving. Serve with the pan juices.

Makes 4 servings

Orzo Stuffing

1½ cups canned low-sodium chicken broth

½ cup orzo

¼ cup chopped shallots

½ cup diced carrots

½ cup diced celery

1 tablespoon olive oil

1 tablespoon butter

2 tablespoons chopped fresh Italian parsley

3 tablespoons grated Parmesan cheese

Salt and freshly ground black pepper to taste

In a medium saucepan, bring the broth to a boil. Add the orzo and cook until all the broth is absorbed, about 7 to 8 minutes. In another saucepan, sauté the shallots, carrots, and celery in the oil and butter until tender. Add the cooked orzo to the sautéed vegetables. Stir in the parsley, Parmesan, salt, and pepper.

Makes 4 servings

Roasted Jerk Pork Tenderloin with Mango Rum Salsa

PUSSER'S RUM RECIPE CONTEST
Grand Prize
Lisa Keevil

Jerk Paste

- 1 teaspoon ground Jamaican allspice
- 1 teaspoon salt
- 1 teaspoon fresh thyme leaves
- 1 tablespoon finely chopped scallions
- ½ teaspoon tamarind paste
- ½ fresh habanero or Scotch bonnet pepper

- 1 teaspoon sugar
- Pinch black pepper
- Pinch ground nutmeg
- Pinch ground cinnamon

- ½ to 2 pounds pork tenderloin
- Mango Rum Salsa (recipe follows)

Preheat the oven to 350 degrees.

Combine all the paste ingredients in a food processor (or mortar and pestle) to make a thick, potent paste. A little goes a long way! Rub the paste over the pork and into the side openings. Place in a shallow baking dish or roasting pan and roast 35 to 45 minutes or to desired temperature. Serve with the salsa.

Makes 4 servings

Mango Rum Salsa

- 2 ripe mangoes, peeled, pitted, and diced
- 3 tablespoons diced red bell pepper

- 1 tablespoon diced yellow bell pepper
- 2½ tablespoons Pusser's Rum
- 2 tablespoons lime juice
- 1 tablespoon sugar

Toss the mangoes with the peppers. Mix together the rum, lime juice, and sugar, then add to mixture. Season to taste. Refrigerate until serving.

Makes about 2 cups

Very Berry Pork Chops

1995 CALIFORNIA STRAWBERRY FESTIVAL'S BERRY-OFF
Grand Prize—Main Dishes
Sue Gulledge
Springville, Alabama

6 boneless pork loin chops (4 to 5 ounces each), all fat removed

3 tablespoons balsamic vinegar

3 tablespoons olive oil

1 teaspoon chopped fresh thyme

4 scallions, chopped (including some green)

½ cup dry white wine

3 tablespoons chopped toasted almonds

8 large ripe but firm strawberries, hulled and chopped

2 large strawberries, for garnish

2 sprigs fresh thyme, for garnish

Marinate the chops in 2 tablespoons of the vinegar and 1 tablespoon of the oil for 15 minutes. Remove from the marinade. In a skillet over medium heat, sauté the pork chops in the remaining 2 tablespoons of oil until done, 5 to 7 minutes on each side (according to the size of the chops). Remove from the pan and keep warm.

In the same skillet, combine the remaining 1 tablespoon vinegar, thyme, and scallions. Cook for 3 minutes, stirring constantly. Add the wine and bring to a boil. Boil 2 minutes. Add the almonds and strawberries; remove from the heat. Drizzle the pork chops with the sauce. Garnish with strawberries and thyme sprigs.

Makes 6 servings

Barbados Grilled Pork with Pineapple Salsa

MARVELOUS MARINADE RECIPE CONTEST
First Place
Priscilla Yee
Concord, California

Marinated Pork

2 teaspoons finely shredded fresh ginger

1½ teaspoons ground allspice

1½ teaspoons curry powder

½ teaspoon cayenne pepper

½ teaspoon ground cinnamon

⅓ cup dark rum

⅓ cup lime juice

¼ cup Worcestershire sauce

2 tablespoons brown sugar

6 lean boneless pork loin chops (about 1½ pounds), cut ¾ inch thick

Pineapple Salsa

2 cups diced pineapple

½ cup diced red bell pepper

½ cup diced scallions

1 tablespoon lime juice

1 tablespoon canola oil

Half-gallon-size pleated Ziploc storage bag
Quart-size Ziploc storage bag

In a half-gallon-size pleated Ziploc storage bag, combine the ginger, allspice, curry powder, cayenne, and cinnamon. Reserve 2 teaspoons of the spice mixture for the salsa. Add the rum, lime juice, Worcestershire sauce, and brown sugar to the remaining spice mixture. Seal the bag and shake to blend. Place the pork chops in the bag; remove excess air, reseal, and turn to coat. Refrigerate 6 to 8 hours.

Meanwhile, combine all the salsa ingredients with the reserved 2 teaspoons spice mixture in a quart-size Ziploc storage bag and refrigerate until ready to cook the pork.

Prepare an outdoor grill.

Remove the pork from the bag and discard the marinade. Grill the pork over medium-hot coals 4 to 5 minutes per side or until the juices run clear, turning once. Serve with the salsa. Garnish with lime wedges, if desired.

Makes 6 servings

Pork Chops Cubano

1997 FIBER ONE RECIPE CONTEST
First Place—Main Dish
Edwina Gadsby
Great Falls, Montana

1 cup Fiber One cereal, crushed
1 tablespoon finely chopped fresh cilantro
2 teaspoons grated orange zest
1 teaspoon finely chopped garlic
1 teaspoon onion powder
1 teaspoon dried oregano

1 teaspoon ground cumin
¼ teaspoon black pepper
4 pork loin chops, cut ½ inch thick (about 1½ pounds)
½ cup buttermilk
Garlic-Citrus Sauce (recipe follows)

Preheat the oven to 400 degrees. Spray a baking sheet with cooking spray.

In a shallow dish, stir together the cereal, cilantro, orange zest, garlic, onion powder, oregano, cumin, and pepper. Dip the pork chops into the buttermilk, then coat completely with the cereal mixture. Place on the baking sheet. Bake 25 to 30 minutes or until the pork is slightly pink when cut near the bone.

While the pork chops are baking, prepare the Garlic-Citrus Sauce; cover and refrigerate until serving time. Serve the pork chops with the sauce.

Makes 4 servings

Garlic-Citrus Sauce

2	teaspoons olive oil	2	tablespoons orange juice
1	tablespoon finely chopped garlic	2	tablespoons chopped fresh cilantro
¼	cup lime juice		

Heat the oil in a small saucepan over medium heat. Add the garlic; cook about 1 minute or until golden, stirring occasionally. Stir in the lime and orange juice. Heat to boiling, stirring occasionally. Remove from the heat; stir in the cilantro.

Makes about ½ cup

Pork Chops with Cranberry-Apple Stuffing and Sauce

CRANEBERRY'S RECIPE CONTEST
First Place—Main Dish
Derolyn St. Louis
Carver, Massachusetts

¼ cup (½ stick) butter

2 tablespoons finely chopped cranberries

1 tablespoon finely chopped onion

1 tablespoon finely chopped celery

½ apple, finely chopped

½ cup bread crumbs

1 teaspoon minced fresh parsley

1 teaspoon minced fresh thyme

½ cup apple juice

2 thick-cut pork chops

Salt and black pepper to taste

Cranberry-Apple Sauce

1 cup cranberries

¼ cup water

1 cup sugar

½ apple, chopped

Preheat the oven to 325 degrees.

In a skillet, melt the butter. Sauté the cranberries, onion, and celery until tender. Add the apple; sauté 1 minute longer. Add the bread crumbs and herbs. Stir in the apple juice and let sit 1 minute. Slice the pork chops horizontally to the bone. Salt and pepper the meat lightly. Stuff with the cranberry-apple mixture and bake for 1 hour.

To make the sauce: Mix all the ingredients in a medium saucepan. Bring to a boil. Gently boil, stirring constantly, 5 minutes. Mash. Serve over the chops.

Makes 2 servings

Craneberry's "Red Gold" Pork Roast

CRANEBERRY'S RECIPE CONTEST
Second Place Entrée
Sue Boucher
South Burlington, Vermont

Mixture 1

1   (14-ounce) can mandarin oranges, drained
2   tablespoons orange marmalade
1   teaspoon cranberry mustard (available in specialty food stores)
1   (5-ounce) bag Craneberry's dried cranberries
½   teaspoon cornstarch
2   cloves garlic, minced

Mixture 2

2   tablespoons orange marmalade
2   tablespoons cranberry mustard
4   large cloves garlic, minced
Salt and pepper to taste

4   pounds pork roast (boneless turkey roast may be substituted)

Preheat the oven to 350 degrees.

Mix the ingredients for Mixtures 1 and 2 in separate bowls and set aside.

Open the roast and pour half of Mixture 1 inside; tie with kitchen string. Rub Mixture 2 over the outside of the meat. Roast for 1 hour. Pour the remainder of Mixture 1 over the meat and continue cooking until done, 15 to 30 minutes. Check the internal temperature. Cut the strings and remove. Slice the roast and serve with the fruit and juices.

Makes 6 servings

Spiced Strawberry-Glazed Roast Pork Tenderloin

1993 CALIFORNIA STRAWBERRY FESTIVAL'S BERRY-OFF
First Place—Main Dish

Robert R. Rogers
Newport, Rhode Island

---

1   cup sugar

1   cup water

1   quart fresh strawberries, hulled

3   tablespoons catsup

⅓   cup cider vinegar

2   tablespoons olive oil

⅛   teaspoon Worcestershire sauce

1   teaspoon chili powder

1   teaspoon paprika

½   teaspoon salt

1   teaspoon onion powder

⅛   teaspoon ground cloves

⅛   teaspoon celery seed

⅛   teaspoon cumin seed

⅛   teaspoon cayenne pepper (optional)

1   to 2 pounds pork tenderloin

Sliced strawberries and parsley sprigs,
   for garnish

Heat the sugar and water to boiling. Cut the strawberries in half and add to the boiling sugar water. Simmer, stir, and mash the strawberries into a thick sauce. Continue to simmer and add the other ingredients except the pork, mixing in each ingredient before adding the next one. Allow the strawberry sauce to cool to room temperature.

Place the pork tenderloin on a large piece of plastic wrap. Spoon enough of the spiced strawberry sauce onto the tenderloin to completely cover it. Wrap the plastic wrap around the sauce-covered tenderloin. Allow it to marinate in the refrigerator for at least 2 hours, preferably overnight.

Preheat the oven to 325 degrees.

Unwrap the marinated tenderloin and place on a rack in a shallow roasting pan. Roast for 45 minutes. Spoon on the strawberry sauce to cover the tenderloin on both sides. Continue to roast for about 45 minutes more. If you use a meat thermometer, the internal temperature should reach 155 degrees. Pork tenderloin should cook about 22 minutes per pound. Remove the roast from the oven and allow it to rest for 10 minutes before serving. Place on a platter garnished with sliced strawberries and parsley.

Makes 4 to 6 servings

Royal Pork Medallions

WATKINS MY FAMILY'S FAVORITE RECIPE CONTEST
Grand Prize
Ellen Burr
Truro, Massachusetts

1 tablespoon Watkins royal pepper, whole

½ cup cider vinegar

1 teaspoon Watkins chicken soup base

1 to 3 tablespoons cornstarch

1 cup water

1½ pounds pork tenderloin, trimmed of fat, cut into 1-inch medallions

1 teaspoon Watkins apple bake seasoning

1 teaspoon Watkins celery salt

2 tablespoons unsalted butter

1 teaspoon Watkins onion liquid spice

¼ cup crabapple jelly or apple jelly

Pickled crabapples or spiced apple rings, for garnish (optional)

Celery leaves, for garnish (optional)

In a small nonreactive saucepan, simmer together the royal pepper and vinegar until the mixture is reduced by half. Combine the chicken soup mix, cornstarch, and water; mix well. Stir this mixture into the reduced vinegar mixture. Bring to a boil, lower the heat, and cook until the mixture is clear and thickens slightly. Remove from the heat and keep warm.

Season the pork with a mixture of the apple bake seasoning and celery salt. In a large heavy or nonstick skillet, melt the butter over high heat. Stir in the onion liquid spice. Add the pork medallions and cook until golden brown on both sides. Stir in the jelly. Cook, turning often, until the meat is well glazed. Do not overcook.

To serve, spoon a small quantity of the royal pepper sauce onto a serving platter. Place the pork medallions on top. Spoon the remaining royal pepper sauce over the pork. Garnish as desired with crabapples and celery leaves. (This dish is especially good with wild rice.)

Makes 6 servings

Side Dishes

Garden Fresh Florentine

SARGENTO "CHEESE MAKES THE RECIPE" CONTEST
First Place—Light Dish
Gloria Piantek
Plainsboro, New Jersey

1 (3½-ounce) pouch boil-in-bag white rice (2 cups cooked)

¼ cup finely chopped onion

1 cup packed coarsely chopped fresh spinach

2 cups thinly sliced zucchini

¼ teaspoon salt

1 cup Sargento Light Ricotta Cheese

½ cup liquid egg substitute, or 2 large eggs

2 tablespoons chopped fresh cilantro

1 cup mild or medium salsa

2 cups (8 ounces) Sargento Light Shredded Mozzarella Cheese

Cook the rice according to package directions; drain well.

Preheat the oven to 375 degrees.

Coat a medium nonstick skillet with nonstick cooking spray. Add the onion and cook over medium-high heat until softened, about 5 minutes, stirring occasionally. Add the spinach; cook 1 minute. Transfer the mixture to a medium bowl; set aside.

Recoat the skillet with cooking spray. Add the zucchini and cook over medium heat until crisp-tender, about 4 minutes, stirring occasionally. Remove from the heat; sprinkle with the salt and set aside. Add the ricotta, egg substitute, and cilantro to the spinach mixture; mix well.

Spread half of the salsa in the bottom of a 10-inch quiche dish or shallow 1½-quart casserole. Spoon half of the rice over the salsa; arrange half of the zucchini over the rice. Top with half of the ricotta mixture. Sprinkle evenly with 1 cup of the mozzarella. Repeat the layering with the remaining rice, zucchini, ½ cup of the mozzarella, and remaining ricotta mixture and salsa. Bake for 20 minutes. Sprinkle with the remaining ½ cup mozzarella. Bake 2 minutes more or until the cheese is melted and the mixture is bubbly.

Makes 4 servings

Classic Cheddar Corn

SARGENTO "CHEESE MAKES THE RECIPE" CONTEST
First Prize—Side Dish
Mrs. Jay E. Baker
Beach City, Ohio

2 tablespoons butter or margarine

2 tablespoons minced onion

1 tablespoon all-purpose flour

1 (16-ounce) package frozen corn kernels

¾ cup low-fat milk

¼ cup finely chopped red bell pepper (optional)

½ teaspoon salt

½ teaspoon sugar

⅛ teaspoon white pepper

1½ cups (6 ounces) Sargento Classic Supreme Shredded Mild Cheddar Cheese

2 tablespoons chopped fresh parsley, for garnish

In a medium saucepan, melt the butter over medium heat. Add the onion; cook 3 minutes, stirring occasionally. Stir in the flour; cook 1 minute, stirring frequently. Add the corn, milk, bell pepper, salt, sugar, and white pepper; bring to a boil over high heat. Reduce the heat to medium-low; cook 5 minutes or until bubbly, stirring occasionally. Stir in the cheddar just until melted. Garnish with parsley.

Makes 6 servings

Moroccan Cheddar Couscous

SARGENTO "CHEESE MAKES THE RECIPE" CONTEST
First Prize—Side Dish
Marie Rizzio
Traverse City, Michigan

1 tablespoon olive oil
1 medium red bell pepper, diced
½ cup chopped onion
2 cloves garlic, minced
1 (14-ounce) can chicken broth

1 cup couscous, uncooked
1½ cups (6 ounces) Sargento Fancy Supreme Shredded Sharp Cheddar Cheese
2 tablespoons chopped fresh cilantro

In a large skillet, heat the oil over medium heat. Add the bell pepper, onion, and garlic; cook 6 minutes or until the vegetables are tender, stirring occasionally. Add the broth; bring to a boil. Stir in the couscous; cover and remove from the heat. Let stand 5 minutes or until the broth is absorbed.

Fluff the couscous mixture with a fork; stir in 1 cup of the cheddar. Sprinkle with the remaining ½ cup cheddar and cilantro.

Makes 4 servings

Sliced Potatoes Lyonnaise

Johnson & Wales University National High School Recipe Contest

Grand Prize—Healthful Dinner Category

Kevin G. Pearce

Glen Allen, Virginia

1 cup chicken stock	2 large baking potatoes, thinly sliced
Cornstarch as needed	¾ large onion crescents, cooked until well caramelized
½ teaspoon minced garlic	¼ cup chopped fresh chives
1 teaspoon coarsely ground black pepper	¼ cup chopped fresh parsley
1 teaspoon salt	

Preheat the oven to 375 degrees. Lightly oil a small casserole.

Thicken the stock with cornstarch. Flavor with the garlic, pepper, and salt. Set aside.

Layer the potatoes, onions, chives, and parsley in the prepared casserole, fanning the potatoes to overlap one another. Pour the stock mixture over the potatoes. Bake for 1½ hours or until tender.

Makes 4 servings

Rocky Top Sweet Potato Casserole

1989 SOUTH CAROLINA POTATO CONTEST
First Place
Rosemary Whitlock
Lancaster, South Carolina

Rocky Top Topping

- 1 cup loosely packed brown sugar
- ½ cup chopped nuts
- ½ cup quick-cooking oats
- ¼ cup (½ stick) butter or margarine, melted

Potato Mixture

- 3 cups mashed cooked sweet potatoes
- 1 cup sugar
- ½ cup (1 stick) butter or margarine, melted
- ⅓ cup milk
- 2 eggs, well beaten
- 1 teaspoon vanilla extract
- ⅓ cup chopped dates (optional)

Preheat the oven to 350 degrees. Lightly butter a 2-quart baking dish.

Combine all the ingredients for the Rocky Top Topping and set aside.

Beat the potatoes with an electric mixer until smooth. Add the remaining ingredients (except the dates) in the order listed and blend with the mixer. Fold in the dates, if desired.

Spoon the mixture into the prepared dish. Cover with the topping and bake for 25 minutes or until the topping is lightly browned.

Makes 6 servings

Bread

Viva La Cinnamon Rolls

BORDEN'S VIVA LIGHT BUTTER HEALTHY REDO RECIPE CONTEST
Overall Contest Winner and Bread Category Winner

Kay Bare
Terreton, Idaho

Dough

1　cup drained cooked white beans
2½ cups warm water
½　cup sugar
2　tablespoons quick-rising yeast
2　eggs, beaten
½　cup powdered milk
2　teaspoons salt
7½ cups all-purpose flour

Filling

½　cup Viva Light Butter, softened
1　cup brown sugar
2　tablespoons ground cinnamon

Glaze

½　cup reconstituted powdered milk
1　tablespoon maple syrup
2　tablespoons Viva Light Butter
1　cup sugar
1　teaspoon vanilla extract

To make the dough: Drain most of the liquid from the beans. Puree in a food processor or blender and transfer to a large bowl. Add the water, sugar, yeast, and eggs; beat until smooth. Add the powdered milk, salt, and 1 cup of the flour and beat for several minutes with a mixer. Add the remaining flour and mix or knead until the dough is firm but soft. (Sometimes a little more flour will have to be added.) Knead for several minutes. Let the dough rise until it doubles in bulk. Punch down and roll out on a surface with little or no flour. You may want to divide the dough and make 2 rounds for easier handling.

To make the filling: Spread the top of the rolled-out dough with the butter and sprinkle evenly with a mixture of the brown sugar and cinnamon. (Optional: You may use nuts, but they do add calories.) Roll up the dough, seal the edges, and slice into 2-inch rolls. Place the rolls, each touching the next, in a baking dish with 2-inch sides. Let rise until almost doubled in bulk, about 20 minutes. Bake the rolls 15 to 18 minutes. Invert the pan onto a baking sheet, cover the bottom of the rolls with foil, and turn right side up.

To make the glaze: Bring the milk, syrup, butter, and sugar to a boil in a small saucepan. Add the vanilla. Reduce the temperature to maintain a soft boil. Cook for 5 minutes, stirring frequently. The mixture will thicken as it cools.

Drizzle the glaze on the warm rolls. Serve warm or cold.

Makes 28 servings

Italian Pesto Oat Rolls

7TH ANNUAL QUAKER OATMEAL
"BAKE IT BETTER WITH OATS" RECIPE CONTEST
First Prize—Bread Category
Mary Louise Lever
Rome, Georgia

1¾ to 2½ cups all-purpose flour

1 cup Quaker oats (quick or old-fashioned), uncooked

½ cup freshly grated Parmesan cheese

2 tablespoons sugar

1 (¼-ounce) package quick-rising yeast (about 2¼ teaspoons)

1¼ teaspoons salt

1 teaspoon fennel seeds, coarsely crushed (optional)

¾ cup water

2 tablespoons olive oil

¼ cup refrigerated pesto sauce

Lightly spray a baking sheet with nonstick cooking spray.

In a large mixing bowl, combine 1¾ cups of the flour, the oats, Parmesan, sugar, yeast, salt, and fennel seeds; mix well. Heat the water and oil until very warm (120 to 130 degrees). Add to the flour mixture. By hand, gradually stir until the dry ingredients are moistened. Stir in enough additional flour to make a soft dough that pulls away from the sides of the bowl.

Knead the dough on a lightly floured surface 5 minutes or until smooth and elastic, lightly sprinkling the work surface and your hands with additional flour if the dough is sticky.

Roll the dough into a 10-inch round. Cut into 12 wedges. Spread about 1 teaspoon pesto across each wedge. Roll up tightly from the wide end. Place the rolls seam side down on the baking sheet; gently push the ends down. Cover with a damp cloth. Let the rolls rise in a warm place 30 minutes.

Meanwhile, preheat the oven to 350 degrees.

Bake the rolls 20 to 22 minutes or until light golden brown. Serve warm.

Makes 12 rolls

Smoky Chipotle Corn Bread

1997 FIBER ONE RECIPE CONTEST
Grand Prize—Breads Category
Helen Wolt
Colorado Springs, Colorado

Helen Wolt

Colorado Springs, Colorado

Helen home-schools her children and enjoys the freedom that allows. She says, "It gives us extra time together and allows us to pursue our individual interests." Now that she is home more, cooking has become her creative outlet. Judging by the great recipes Helen creates, her family must really enjoy spending time in the kitchen. Helen also exercises regularly, plays the piano, and collects antique quilts and children's books.

1   cup Fiber One cereal
1   cup cornmeal
1   cup all-purpose flour
2   teaspoons baking powder
1   teaspoon baking soda
1   teaspoon salt
1   teaspoon chili powder

1¼ cups buttermilk
1   egg, or ¼ cup fat-free egg product
¼   cup barbecue sauce
2   tablespoons vegetable oil
2   tablespoons minced chipotle peppers packed in adobo sauce

Preheat the oven to 400 degrees. Spray an 8- or 9-inch square baking pan with non-stick cooking spray.

In a large bowl, combine the dry ingredients. Make a well in the center. Blend together the wet ingredients, add to the well, then stir into the flour mixture. Pour into the baking pan. Bake 25 to 30 minutes or until golden brown. Serve warm.

Makes 9 servings

Italian Herbed Oatmeal Focaccia

QUAKER OATMEAL "BAKE IT BETTER WITH OATS" RECIPE CONTEST
First Prize—Muffin/Bread Category
Edwina Gadsby
Great Falls, Montana

2 tablespoons cornmeal	2 teaspoons sugar
1½ to 2¼ cups all-purpose flour	1½ teaspoons garlic salt
1 cup Quaker oats (quick or old-fashioned), uncooked	1 cup water
2 tablespoons Italian seasoning	¼ cup plus 2 tablespoons olive oil
1 (¼-ounce) package quick-rising yeast (2¼ teaspoons)	4 to 6 oil-pack sun-dried tomatoes, drained and chopped
	¼ cup grated Parmesan cheese

Lightly spray a 13x9-inch baking pan with nonstick cooking spray; dust with the cornmeal.

In a large bowl, combine 1 cup of the flour, the oats, 1 tablespoon of the Italian seasoning, the yeast, the sugar, and 1 teaspoon of the garlic salt; mix well.

In a small saucepan, heat the water and ¼ cup of the oil until very warm (120 to 130 degrees); stir into the flour mixture. Gradually stir in enough of the remaining flour to make a soft dough. Turn the dough out onto a lightly floured surface. Knead 8 to 10 minutes or until smooth and elastic. Cover and let rest 10 minutes.

Pat dough into the prepared pan, pressing it out to the edges of the pan. Using your fingertips, poke indentations all over the surface of the dough; brush with the remaining 2 tablespoons oil. Sprinkle with the remaining 1 tablespoon Italian seasoning and ½ teaspoon garlic salt. Arrange the dried tomatoes across the top; sprinkle with the Parmesan. Cover and let rise in a warm place until doubled in bulk, about 30 minutes.

Meanwhile, preheat the oven to 400 degrees.

Bake the focaccia 25 to 30 minutes or until golden brown. Cut into strips or squares. Serve warm.

Makes 12 servings

Quick Cheese Date-Nut Scones

SARGENTO "CHEESE MAKES THE RECIPE" CONTEST 1996
First Place—Side Dish
Joyce L. Bowman
Raleigh, North Carolina

2 cups reduced-fat buttermilk biscuit baking mix

¼ cup (½ stick) chilled unsalted butter, cut in bits

1½ cups (6 ounces) Sargento 3 Cheese Gourmet Cheddar Recipe Blend

1 cup chopped pitted dates or raisins

1 cup chopped walnuts

1 cup plain low-fat yogurt

Honey Butter

½ cup unsalted butter, softened

2 tablespoons honey

Preheat the oven to 425 degrees. Oil a baking sheet well.

Place the baking mix in a medium bowl; cut in the butter with a pastry blender or 2 knives until the mixture is the size of small peas. Stir in the cheese, dates, and walnuts; mix well. Add the yogurt; mix well.

Mound the dough on the prepared baking sheet. With floured hands, pat the dough into a 9-inch round. Bake 12 to 16 minutes or until golden brown. Let stand 10 minutes; cut into 8 wedges.

While the scones are cooking, make the honey butter: Beat the butter and honey with a fork until light and fluffy.

Serve the scones warm with the honey butter.

Makes 8 scones

North Country Rosemary Olive Scones

4TH ANNUAL QUAKER OATMEAL "BAKE IT BETTER WITH OATS" RECIPE CONTEST

First Place—Bread/Muffin Category

Virginia Moon

Harvest, Alabama

Virginia Moon

Harvest, Alabama

Virginia had her first big win in 1989 during a contest sponsored by the Florida Tomato Growers and Weight Watchers. She and her husband, Rodney, raise soybeans and cotton on their farm, Moon Acres. Virginia has a rink and loves to ride her horse, Emily, in dressage competitions. To stay in shape, she runs, bikes, and lifts weights. Always careful about her diet, Virginia specializes in taking familiar old recipes and reinventing them by making them healthier and quicker.

½ cup all-purpose flour

1 cup Quaker oats (quick or old-fashioned), uncooked

1 tablespoon sugar

2 teaspoons baking powder

½ teaspoon chopped fresh rosemary, or ½ teaspoon dried, crushed

¾ teaspoon black pepper

½ teaspoon salt (optional)

½ cup (1 stick) chilled butter or margarine

⅓ cup half-and-half or milk

2 eggs, slightly beaten

⅓ cup coarsely chopped pitted Kalamata or ripe olives

Preheat the oven to 425 degrees. Lightly oil a baking sheet.

In a large bowl, combine the flour, oats, sugar, baking powder, rosemary, pepper, and salt (if desired). Cut in the butter with a pastry blender or 2 knives until the mixture resembles coarse crumbs. Combine the remaining ingredients, add to the flour mixture, and mix just until the dry ingredients are moistened.

Turn the dough out onto a lightly floured surface; knead 8 to 10 times. Pat the dough into an 8-inch round about ¾ inch thick; cut into 8 wedges. Place the wedges on the prepared baking sheet. Bake 18 to 20 minutes or until light golden brown. Serve warm.

Makes 8 scones

Charleston Four-Corner Biscuits

RED BAND FLOUR RECIPE CONTEST
First Place
Don Campagna
Summerville, South Carolina

2 cups Red Band All-Purpose Flour	¼ cup sugar
2 teaspoons baking powder	½ cup (1 stick) chilled margarine, cut in bits
½ teaspoon baking soda	
½ teaspoon salt	¾ cup nonfat buttermilk

Preheat the oven to 470 degrees. Line a 13x9-inch baking sheet with foil.

In a large bowl, mix the dry ingredients with a fork. Cut in the margarine and then stir in the buttermilk until the dough is stiff. With floured hands, knead in the bowl until almost all of the flour is incorporated, then turn out on a floured counter and knead for 2 minutes.

Lay floured waxed paper on the counter and transfer the dough to it. With floured hands, gently press the dough into a 12x8-inch rectangle ½ inch thick. Then lift the edges of the waxed paper and fold the short ends into the middle, forming 2 layers of dough. Divide the resulting 8x6-inch rectangle into 2-inch square biscuits by cutting the dough halfway through with a cold serrated bread knife.

Invert the foil-lined baking sheet lengthwise over the dough. Wrap the edges of the waxed paper around the baking sheet and quickly flip the dough over. Peel the waxed paper off and score the top of the inverted dough with lines that correspond to the previous cuts. Bake 15 minutes.

Makes 12 biscuits

Cran-Apple Oatmeal Swirl Rolls

**8TH ANNUAL QUAKER OATMEAL "BAKE IT BETTER WITH OATS"
RECIPE CONTEST**

First Prize—Bread/Muffin Category

Jeanne Holt

Mendota Heights, Minnesota

Rolls

- 1½ to 2 cups all-purpose flour
- ⅔ cup Quaker oats (quick or old-fashioned), uncooked
- ¼ cup firmly packed brown sugar
- 1 (¼-ounce) package quick-rising yeast (about 2¼ teaspoons)
- ½ teaspoon salt
- ½ cup warm milk or water (110 to 115 degrees)
- ¼ cup (½ stick) margarine or butter, melted
- 1 egg, lightly beaten

Filling and Topping

- ⅔ cup chopped walnuts or pecans
- ½ cup firmly packed brown sugar
- ⅓ cup (5 tablespoons plus 1 teaspoon) margarine or butter, melted
- ⅓ cup Quaker oats (quick or old-fashioned), uncooked
- 2 teaspoons apple pie spice or ground cinnamon
- ⅓ cup chopped dried apples
- ⅓ cup dried cranberries
- 1 tablespoon all-purpose flour

Lightly grease an 8- or 9-inch square baking pan.

To make the rolls: Combine 1½ cups of the flour, the oats, brown sugar, yeast, and salt in a large mixing bowl. Add the milk, margarine, and egg; beat at medium speed 2 minutes. Stir in enough of the remaining flour to make a soft dough that pulls away from the sides of the bowl.

Knead the dough on a lightly floured surface 5 minutes or until smooth and elastic, lightly sprinkling the work surface and your hands with additional flour if the dough is sticky. Cover loosely with plastic wrap while preparing the filling.

To make the filling: Combine the walnuts, brown sugar, margarine, oats, and apple pie spice in a small bowl; mix well. Reserve ⅓ cup; set aside. Add the apples and cranberries to the remaining oat mixture; mix well.

Roll the dough into a 16x8-inch rectangle. Sprinkle the apple mixture evenly over the dough; press firmly into the dough. Starting at a long end, roll the dough up tightly; pinch the seam to seal. Cut the dough crosswise into 12 slices. Place the slices, cut side down, in the prepared pan; cover. Let the rolls rise in a warm place until almost doubled in bulk, about 30 minutes.

Preheat the oven to 350 degrees. Combine the reserved ⅓ cup oat mixture with the remaining 1 tablespoon flour; sprinkle evenly over the rolls. Bake 30 to 35 minutes or until golden brown. Let cool 5 minutes in the pan on a wire rack. Turn out onto a platter. Serve warm.

Makes 12 rolls

Peppered Parmesan Breadsticks

1997 FIBER ONE RECIPE CONTEST
First Prize—Breads
Edwina Gadsby
Great Falls, Montana

1 cup warm water (105 to 115 degrees)

1 (¼-ounce) package active dry yeast

1 tablespoon sugar

1 cup Fiber One cereal, crushed

2¼ cups Gold Medal all-purpose flour

½ cup grated Parmesan cheese

1½ teaspoons grated lemon zest

1 teaspoon garlic salt

1 teaspoon coarsely ground black pepper

¼ to ½ teaspoon ground red pepper (cayenne)

2 tablespoons olive oil

Cornmeal

1 egg white, slightly beaten

Stir together the water, yeast, and sugar. Let stand 5 minutes.

Place the cereal, flour, Parmesan, lemon zest, garlic salt, black pepper, and red pepper in a food processor. Cover and process about 10 seconds or until blended. Add the oil; cover and process 10 seconds. Add the yeast mixture; cover and process, using quick pulses, until the dough forms a ball. Let rest 5 minutes. Cover and process 10 seconds. Remove the dough to a bowl; cover and let rise 10 minutes.

Preheat the oven to 325 degrees. Spray 2 baking sheets with cooking spray.

Divide the dough into 16 equal pieces. On a surface sprinkled with cornmeal, roll each piece of dough into a thin rope about 14 inches long. Place on the baking sheets. Brush with the egg white; sprinkle with additional ground black and red pepper, if desired. Let stand 15 minutes. Bake 25 to 35 minutes or until golden brown and crisp. Let cool on wire rack.

Makes 16 breadsticks

Mauna Loa Bread with Mac Nut Honey Butter

SECOND ANNUAL MAUNA LOA MACADAMIA NUT CONTEST
Grand Prize
Elaine Harai
Captain Cook, Hawaii

1   (¼-ounce) package active dry yeast
¼   cup warm water (about 110 degrees)
½   cup sugar
1   tablespoon grated lemon zest
⅓   cup warm milk (about 110 degrees)
½   teaspoon salt
5   eggs

½   cup Mauna Loa Macadamia Nuts, diced small
5½ to 6 cups all-purpose flour
1   egg beaten with 1 tablespoon milk

Mac Nut Honey Butter

½   cup butter, softened
¼   cup macadamia nut honey

In a large bowl, dissolve the yeast in the warm water. Blend in the butter, sugar, lemon zest, milk, salt, eggs, and nuts. Gradually beat in 5 cups of the flour to make a stiff dough.

Turn the dough out onto a floured board and knead until smooth and satiny (10 to 15 minutes), adding more flour as needed to prevent sticking. Place the dough in a greased bowl; turn over to grease the top. Cover and let rise in a warm place until doubled in bulk, about 2 hours.

Punch the dough down, then knead briefly on a floured board to release the air. Return to the greased bowl; turn the dough over. Cover with plastic wrap and refrigerate for at least 1 hour or as long as 24 hours.

Select a 2- to 2½-quart mixing bowl of ovenproof glass or metal (about 9 inches in diameter and 4 inches deep). Wrap the outside with foil, folding excess foil inside bowl. Oil the foil generously and invert the bowl on an oiled 15x12-inch baking sheet.

Punch the dough down, knead briefly on a floured board, and divide into 20 equal pieces. Working with 2 pieces at a time (keep remaining dough covered and refrigerated), roll each piece into a rope about ⅜ inch thick and 18 to 20 inches long. Pinch the ends of 2 ropes to seal, then twist the ropes together.

Starting at the bowl rim, wrap the twists around the bowl, pinching ends together to join whenever you add a new twist. Keep the bowl in the refrigerator to prevent uneven rising as you roll more ropes. Lightly cover the shaped dough with plastic wrap and let rise in a warm place until puffy, 20 to 30 minutes.

Preheat the oven to 350 degrees.

Gently brush the dough with the egg mixture. Bake 25 to 30 minutes or until well browned. Let cool on a rack for about 10 minutes.

Crumple a large piece of foil into a loose ball with the same diameter and depth as the bowl; set the foil ball in the center of a rack. Gently remove the bread from the bowl, using a small spatula if needed to free it. Set the bread over the foil so that the foil supports the top of the loaf (bread is fragile when hot) until it is almost cool.

To make the honey butter: Beat the butter with the honey until fluffy. Serve with the bread.

Makes 1 bowl-shaped loaf

Savory Pull-Apart Bread

BISQUICK CONTEST
First Place—Breads
Helen Conwell
Fairhope, Alabama

Helen Conwell

Fairhope, Alabama

As a young girl, Helen had two goals. First, she wanted to be a medical doctor like her father, and second, she wanted to have the opportunity to travel the world. She has achieved both. Upon completion of medical school, Helen lived in Venezuela for six years and then spent three years in Trinidad. Even though she now claims to be retired, Helen is certainly active in cooking contesting. Besides the joy of her grandchildren, Helen also finds pleasure in reading, gardening, and painting.

1   medium red bell pepper (see Note)

10 halves sun-dried tomatoes (not oil-packed), finely chopped

2   cups Bisquick Original baking mix

1   (8-ounce) package feta cheese, coarsely crumbled

¾ cup milk

1   tablespoon chopped fresh oregano, or 1 teaspoon dried

1   tablespoon chopped fresh basil, or 1 teaspoon dried

1   clove garlic, finely chopped

2   tablespoons olive or vegetable oil

Preheat the broiler.

Broil the bell pepper 5 inches from the heat, turning occasionally, until the skin is blistered and evenly browned but not burned. Place in a plastic bag; close tightly. Let stand 20 minutes. Peel the skin from the pepper and discard; finely chop the pepper.

Cover the dried tomatoes with boiling water. Let stand 10 minutes; drain.

Preheat the oven to 425 degrees. Lightly spray a 9-inch square baking pan with non-stick cooking spray.

Mix the baking mix, tomatoes, half of the feta, and the milk in a medium bowl. Mix the remaining feta, bell pepper, oregano, basil, garlic, and oil in a small bowl.

Drop half of the dough by tablespoonfuls closely together in an irregular pattern in the pan. Spoon half of the feta mixture over the dough. Drop the remaining dough over the feta mixture. Top with the remaining feta mixture. Bake about 20 minutes or until golden. Serve warm.

Makes 4 to 6 servings

Note: 1 cup jarred roasted red bell peppers, drained and chopped, can be substituted for the bell pepper; omit the broiling step.

Warm Praline 'n' Cream Muffins

QUAKER OATS "IT'S THE RIGHT THING TO DO" RECIPE CONTEST
First Place—Breads/Muffins
Martha Davis
Inman, South Carolina

Martha Davis

Inman, South Carolina

Martha and her husband, Walter, are retired and live on a lake. Boating, fishing, and water sports are natural pastimes for her large, close family. I am sure they all enjoy it when she makes Warm Praline 'n' Cream Muffins. Martha tries to walk four miles a day with her neighbors and is active in the food pantry her church operates.

½ cup firmly packed brown sugar

⅓ cup (5⅓ tablespoons) margarine or butter, softened

1 (3-ounce) package cream cheese, softened

⅔ cup milk

1 egg

1 teaspoon maple or vanilla extract

1 cup Quaker oats (quick or old-fashioned), uncooked

½ cup all-purpose flour

⅓ cup whole wheat flour

1 tablespoon baking powder

½ teaspoon salt (optional)

¾ cup chopped pecans

Preheat the oven to 400 degrees. Oil only the bottoms of 12 standard muffin cups or line with paper baking cups.

In a medium bowl, beat the brown sugar, margarine, and cream cheese until creamy. Add the milk, egg, and maple extract; mix well.

Combine the flours, baking powder, salt (if desired), and ½ cup of the pecans. Add to the wet mixture and stir just until the dry ingredients are moistened. Fill the prepared muffin cups three-quarters full. Sprinkle with the remaining ¼ cup pecans. Bake 20 to 22 minutes or until golden brown. Let cool; serve slightly warm.

To freeze the muffins, wrap securely; seal, label, and freeze.

To reheat frozen muffins, unwrap and microwave on high about 45 seconds per muffin.

Makes 12 muffins

Very Cheddar Cranberry Muffin Tops

SARGENTO "CHEESE MAKES THE RECIPE" CONTEST
First Prize—Appetizers & Snacks—$1,000
Irene E. Souza
Cupertino, California

2½ cups buttermilk biscuit baking mix

1½ cups (6 ounces) Sargento Fancy Supreme Shredded Sharp Cheddar Cheese

⅓ cup sugar

¼ teaspoon ground cloves

½ cup cranberry-orange relish

⅓ cup milk

2 tablespoons butter or margarine, melted and cooled

1 egg

Glaze

1 cup confectioner's sugar

1 tablespoon cranberry-orange relish

1½ to 2 tablespoons milk

Preheat the oven to 375 degrees. Lightly oil 2 baking sheets. In a large bowl, stir together the baking mix, cheddar, sugar, and cloves. In a medium bowl, combine the relish, milk, butter, and egg; mix well. Add to the dry ingredients, stirring just until the dry ingredients are moistened (batter should be lumpy). Drop the batter by level ⅓ cup measure onto the baking sheets, spacing 2 inches apart. Bake 20 to 22 minutes or until golden brown.

Meanwhile, prepare the glaze: In a small bowl, combine the confectioner's sugar, relish, and enough milk to make a drizzling consistency.

Transfer the muffin tops to a cooling rack set over a sheet of waxed paper; drizzle the glaze over the muffin tops. Serve warm or at room temperature.

Makes 8 to 10 muffin tops

Tip: Muffins may be stored, tightly covered, at room temperature up to 3 days or frozen up to 3 months.

Key West Black-Eyed Pea Cakes

WHITE LILY CORNMEAL RECIPE CONTEST
First Place—Breads & Muffins
Virginia Moon
Harvest, Alabama

1 to 1¼ cups White Lily Self-Rising Cornmeal Mix

¼ cup White Lily All-Purpose Soft Wheat Flour

1 teaspoon sugar

2 cups milk

1 cup cooked black-eyed peas, coarsely mashed

1 egg

2 tablespoons grated onion

2 tablespoons chopped fresh cilantro

2 cloves garlic, minced

⅛ teaspoon hot pepper sauce

1 cup sour cream

1 cup salsa

Preheat a lightly greased griddle.

In a mixing bowl, combine the cornmeal mix, flour, and sugar. Add the milk, black-eyed peas, egg, onion, cilantro, garlic, and hot sauce. Stir just until dry ingredients are moistened. Let the batter stand 5 minutes.

Pour about 2 tablespoons batter onto the hot griddle. Cook until browned on both sides, turning to cook the second side when the surface bubbles and the edges are slightly dry. Serve with sour cream and salsa.

Makes 6 servings

Desserts

White Chocolate Strawberry Dream Pie

DARIGOLD'S QUICK FIXIN'S WITH MIX-INS CONTEST
First Place
Edwina Gadsby
Great Falls, Montana

Edwina Gadsby

Great Falls, Montana

"White Chocolate Strawberry Dream Pie is a variation of a white chocolate cheesecake that I developed and have made for the holidays for years. I sometimes make it even more decadent by serving caramel sauce with it." Edwina began contesting in 1993 by winning a trip to Governor's Inn in Vermont in the first contest she entered. Since then she has been winning regularly. Edwina credits her success to her love for experimenting in the kitchen. Having personally made this recipe many times, I can attest that this is an experiment that was really a success.

1   quart Darigold Strawberry Ice Cream, softened

3   tablespoons almond-flavored liqueur, or 2 teaspoons almond extract

1   purchased 8-inch butter-flavored or graham cracker pie crust

1¼ cups Darigold Whipping Cream

1   cup (6 ounces) chopped white chocolate or vanilla milk chips

White chocolate curls and/or fresh strawberries, for garnish (optional)

Combine the ice cream and almond liqueur; stir until well blended. Spread evenly in the pie crust; freeze.

Microwave ¼ cup of the cream and the white chocolate on high 2 minutes or until chocolate is almost melted, stirring every 45 seconds until smooth.

Beat the remaining cream until soft peaks form. Fold half of the whipped cream into the white chocolate mixture. Fold in the remaining whipped cream until blended.

Remove the pie from the freezer. Spoon or pipe the white chocolate mousse over the top of the ice cream. Cover and freeze at least 1 hour.

Place the pie in the refrigerator 10 minutes before serving. Garnish with white chocolate curls or strawberry slices, if desired.

Makes 8 servings

"Fried" Ice Cream Sundae

DARIGOLD QUICK FIXIN'S WITH MIX-INS CONTEST
Grand Prize
Irene E. Souza
Cupertino, California

1   quart Darigold Vanilla Ice Cream
¼   cup Darigold Butter
½   cup packed brown sugar

3   cups crushed toasted corn, wheat, or rice cereal
1   (12-ounce) jar chocolate fudge ice cream topping

Scoop the ice cream into 6 balls using a ⅔-cup ice cream scoop; place on a baking sheet and freeze until solid.

Melt the butter in a heavy skillet; stir in the crushed cereal. Remove the ice cream balls from the freezer and roll in the cereal mixture until coated. Return to the baking sheet and freezer until ready to serve.

To serve, place the balls on individual serving plates; drizzle with topping. Serve immediately.

Makes 6 servings

Tropical Lime Oat Bars

7TH ANNUAL QUAKER OATMEAL "BAKE IT BETTER WITH OATS"
RECIPE CONTEST
First Prize—Cookie Category
Helen Wolt
Colorado Springs, Colorado

¾ cup sugar

½ cup (1 stick) butter or margarine, softened

2 cups Quaker oats (quick or old-fashioned), uncooked

1¼ cups all-purpose flour

½ teaspoon salt (optional)

1 (14-ounce) can low-fat sweetened condensed milk (not evaporated)

½ cup reduced-fat sour cream

½ cup fresh lime juice (from 3 limes)

2 teaspoons firmly packed finely grated lime zest (from 2 to 3 limes)

½ cup shredded sweetened coconut

1 (3½-ounce) jar macadamia nuts, chopped (about ¾ cup)

Preheat the oven to 350 degrees. Lightly oil a 13x9-inch baking pan with nonstick cooking spray.

In a large bowl, beat the sugar and butter until creamy. Add the combined oats, flour, and salt; mix until crumbly. Reserve 1 cup of the mixture for the topping; set aside. Press the remaining oat mixture onto the bottom of the baking pan. Bake 10 minutes.

In the same bowl, combine the condensed milk, sour cream, lime juice, and lime zest; mix well. Pour evenly over the crust.

Combine the reserved oat mixture with the coconut and nuts; mix well. Sprinkle evenly over the filling; lightly pat the topping into the filling.

Bake 30 to 34 minutes or until the topping is light golden brown. Cool completely before cutting into bars. Store, covered, in the refrigerator.

Makes 32 bars

Maple Pecan Oatmeal Bars

7TH ANNUAL QUAKER OATMEAL "BAKE IT BETTER WITH OATS"
RECIPE CONTEST
Grand Prize
Karen Gonzales
Glendale, Arizona

Bars

¾ cup (1½ sticks) butter or margarine

2¼ cups Quaker oats (quick or old-fashioned), uncooked

2 cups all-purpose flour

1½ cups firmly packed brown sugar

¾ cup shredded sweetened coconut (optional)

1 teaspoon baking soda

¼ teaspoon salt (optional)

⅓ cup maple-flavored pancake syrup

1 egg, lightly beaten

1 teaspoon vanilla extract

Topping

1½ cups chopped pecans (about 6 ounces)

¼ cup firmly packed brown sugar

⅓ cup maple-flavored pancake syrup

Preheat the oven to 350 degrees. Lightly spray a 13x9-inch baking pan with nonstick cooking spray.

To make the bars: Melt the butter; set aside to cool. In a large bowl, combine the oats, flour, brown sugar, coconut, baking soda, and salt; mix well. In a small bowl, combine the melted butter, syrup, egg, and vanilla; mix well. Add to the oat mixture; mix well (dough will be stiff). Press the dough evenly onto the bottom of the pan.

To make the topping: Combine the pecans and brown sugar in a small bowl. Sprinkle evenly over the dough; press down lightly. Drizzle the syrup evenly over the pecans.

Bake 35 to 38 minutes or until the edges are set but the middle is soft. (Do not overbake.) Let cool completely in the pan on a wire rack. Cut into bars. Store tightly covered.

Makes 32 bars

3D Brownies

BAKER'S CHOCOLATE NATIONAL BEST BROWNIE RECIPE CONTEST
"Best of the Best" & "Serious Chocolate" Category Winner
LoriAnn Glen
Overland, Missouri

Brownie Layer

1 (8-ounce) package Baker's semi-sweet baking chocolate squares

3 tablespoons butter or margarine

2 eggs

1¼ cups sugar

¼ cup water

1 teaspoon vanilla extract

1 cup all-purpose flour

1 teaspoon Calumet baking powder

¼ teaspoon salt

¾ cup chopped toasted macadamia nuts

Cheesecake Layer

1 (8-ounce) package Philadelphia Brand cream cheese, softened

⅔ cup sugar

2 eggs

1 tablespoon lemon juice

1 teaspoon vanilla extract

2 tablespoons all-purpose flour

Glaze

⅓ cup heavy cream

6 squares Baker's semisweet baking chocolate, finely chopped

¼ cup chopped toasted macadamia nuts

Preheat the oven to 350 degrees. Line a 13x9-inch baking pan with foil and oil the foil.

To make the brownie layer: Microwave the chocolate and butter in a large microwavable bowl on high 2 minutes or until the chocolate is almost melted. Beat the eggs in a separate large bowl with an electric mixer on medium speed until foamy. Gradually beat in the sugar, water, and vanilla until thick and lemon colored. Beat in the chocolate mixture. Stir in the flour, baking powder, salt, and nuts. Spread half of the brownie batter into the prepared baking pan; set aside.

To make the cheesecake layer: Beat the cream cheese, sugar, eggs, lemon juice, and vanilla in a medium bowl with an electric mixer until smooth. Mix in the flour. Spread evenly over the brownie batter in the pan. Spread the remaining brownie batter evenly over the cream cheese layer. Swirl through the batter with a knife to marbleize.

Bake 45 to 50 minutes or until a toothpick inserted in the center comes out with fudgy crumbs. *Do not overbake.* Let cool in the pan.

To make the glaze: Microwave the cream in a medium microwavable bowl on high 45 seconds or until simmering. Stir in the chopped chocolate until the chocolate is melted and the mixture is smooth. Spread the glaze over the cooled brownies. Sprinkle with the nuts.

Refrigerate 1 hour or until the glaze is set. Cut into 24 squares.

Makes 24 brownies

Heaven Sent-Sations

INTERBAKE DAIRY ICE CREAM SANDWICH SENSATIONS
RECIPE CONTEST
Second Prize
Connie Snyder
Hammond, Indiana

5 to 6 (2½-ounce) Ice Cream Sandwiches

1 (3-ounce) package cream cheese, softened

1 teaspoon vanilla extract

1 cup confectioner's sugar

1 (8-ounce) container frozen whipped topping, thawed

10 peanut butter sandwich cookies, crushed

Chocolate shavings or chocolate shot, for garnish

Place the ice cream sandwiches side by side in an 8-inch square baking dish. (You may cut the sandwiches to fit. Don't worry about spaces.) Place the pan in the freezer.

Beat the cream cheese until smooth; add the vanilla and confectioner's sugar; mix well. Fold the whipped topping and crushed cookies into the cream cheese mixture. Spread this mixture over the ice cream sandwiches, filling any gaps between the sandwiches. Sprinkle with the chocolate shavings or chocolate shot. Return to freezer for ½ to 2 hours or until frozen. Cut into 9 squares.

Makes 9 servings

Chocolate Marshmallow Sandwich Bars

INTERBAKE DAIRY ICE CREAM SANDWICH SENSATIONS RECIPE CONTEST
First Prize—Adult Category
Joan Vaccaro
Pompton Lakes, New Jersey

5⅓ (2½-ounce) Ice Cream Sandwiches
½ cup creamy peanut butter
½ cup light corn syrup
⅓ cup evaporated milk
1 (12-ounce) package semisweet chocolate chips

2 teaspoons vanilla extract
⅓ cup marshmallow creme
½ cup chopped walnuts
½ cup white chocolate morsels

Place the ice cream sandwiches in a single layer in an 8-inch square baking pan. Spread the peanut butter in an even layer over the ice cream sandwiches. Place in the freezer until needed.

In a 2-quart saucepan, combine the corn syrup, evaporated milk, chocolate chips, and vanilla. Cook over low heat, stirring, until the mixture is smooth.

Remove the pan from the freezer; pour the hot mixture over the peanut butter layer. Quickly spoon the marshmallow creme on top. Take a knife and swirl the marshmallow creme into the chocolate mixture. (Since the mixture is hot, the creme will spread easily.) Sprinkle with the nuts and white morsels. Freeze 4 hours or until firm. Cut into 8 bars.

Makes 8 servings

Fat-Free Peach Frozen Yogurt

EAGLE BRAND LOW FAT AND FAT FREE "SIGNATURE DESSERTS" RECIPE CONTEST

Grand Prize

Thomas Kelly

Phoenix, Arizona

1   (16-ounce) container plain fat-free yogurt

2   cups pureed fresh or frozen peaches

1   (14-ounce) can Eagle Brand Fat Free Sweetened Condensed Skimmed Milk (not evaporated milk)

1   cup skim milk

2   tablespoons vanilla extract

In an ice cream freezer container, combine all the ingredients; mix well. Freeze according to manufacturer's instructions. Freeze any leftovers.

Makes about 2 quarts

Tip: Recipe can be doubled.

Caramel Ribbon Brownies

T. Marzetti's Caramel Apple Dip Contest
Second Place
Margaret Blakely
New Phil, Ohio

1 (21.5-ounce) package brownie mix
½ cup butter or margarine, softened
⅓ cup plus ¼ cup creamy peanut butter
3 eggs
2 (8-ounce) packages cream cheese, softened

1 cup sugar
3 tablespoons all-purpose flour
¼ cup sour cream
2 teaspoons vanilla extract
⅔ cup T. Marzetti's Old Fashioned Caramel Apple Dip
1 tablespoon hot water

Preheat the oven to 325 degrees. Oil the bottom of a 13x9-inch baking pan.

In a bowl, combine the brownie mix, margarine, ¼ cup peanut butter, and 1 egg. Beat until the mixture forms a dough. Press on the bottom of the prepared pan.

In large mixer bowl, beat the cream cheese and ⅓ cup peanut butter until smooth. Add the sugar, flour, sour cream, and vanilla; mix well. Beat in the remaining 2 eggs just until blended. Spread over the brownie mixture in the pan.

Stir together the caramel apple dip and hot water until well blended. Drop by the ½ teaspoon over the cream cheese layer. With a table knife, cut through the mixtures to swirl the caramel through the entire filling.

Bake 35 to 45 minutes or until the center is set. Let cool. Store, covered, in the refrigerator.

Makes 24 brownies

Peanut Butter 'n' Fudge Filled Bars

4TH ANNUAL QUAKER OATMEAL
"BAKE IT BETTER WITH OATS" RECIPE CONTEST
Grand Prize
Paula McHargue
Richmond, Kentucky

Paula McHargue

Lexington, Kentucky

Paula shares her hobbies with husband Richard, himself a successful contester. The two are award-winning cloggers as well. The couple have built a house on the farm her parents owned when she was born. Her roots in the community run back to the time her ancestors helped settle nearby Boonesboro with its famous namesake, Daniel Boone. In her spare time Paula performs with a dance troupe at fundraisers, as well as schools and nursing homes.

2 cups firmly packed brown sugar

1 cup (2 sticks) butter or margarine, softened

¼ cup plus 2 tablespoons peanut butter

2 eggs

2 cups all-purpose flour

1 teaspoon baking soda

¼ teaspoon salt (optional)

2 cups Quaker oats (quick or old-fashioned), uncooked

1 (14-ounce) can sweetened condensed milk

1 (12-ounce) package semisweet chocolate chips (2 cups)

⅔ cup chopped pecans

Preheat the oven to 350 degrees. Grease a 13x9-inch baking pan.

In a large mixer bowl, beat the brown sugar, butter, and ¼ cup peanut butter until light and fluffy. Beat in the eggs. Combine the flour, baking soda, and salt. Add to the butter mixture; beat until well mixed. Stir in the oats; mix well. Reserve 1 cup of the mixture; set aside. Spread the remaining oat mixture evenly in the prepared pan.

In a small saucepan, combine the condensed milk, chocolate chips, and remaining 2 tablespoons peanut butter. Cook over low heat until the chocolate is melted, stirring constantly. Remove from the heat; stir in the pecans. Spread this mixture evenly over the mixture in the pan. Drop the reserved oat mixture by teaspoonfuls evenly over the chocolate mixture. Bake 25 to 30 minutes or until light golden brown. Let cool completely on wire rack. Cut into bars.

Makes 32 bars

Fudgy Bonbons

36TH PILLSBURY BAKE-OFF CONTEST
Grand Prize
Mary A. Tyndall
Whiteville, North Carolina

1	(12-ounce) package semisweet chocolate chips
¼	cup (½ stick) butter or margarine
1	(14-ounce) can sweetened condensed milk (not evaporated)
2	cups Pillsbury BEST All Purpose or Unbleached Flour
½	cup finely chopped nuts (optional)

1	teaspoon vanilla extract
60	milk chocolate candy kisses or white- and chocolate-striped candy kisses, unwrapped
2	ounces white baking bar or vanilla-flavored candy coating
1	teaspoon shortening or oil

Preheat the oven to 350 degrees.

In a medium saucepan, combine the chocolate chips and butter; cook and stir over very low heat until the chips are melted and smooth. Add the condensed milk; mix well.

In a medium bowl, combine the flour, nuts (if desired), chocolate mixture, and vanilla; mix well. Shape 1 tablespoonful (use a measuring spoon) of dough around each candy kiss, covering completely. Place 1 inch apart on ungreased baking sheets.

Bake for 6 to 8 minutes. The cookies will be soft and appear shiny but become firm as they cool. *Do not overbake.* Remove from the baking sheets; let cool.

In a small saucepan, combine the white baking bar and shortening; cook and stir over low heat until melted and smooth. Drizzle over the cookies. Store in a tightly covered container.

Makes 5 dozen cookies

Maui Macadamia Macaroons

PREMIUM SALTINE "BLUE RIBBON" RECIPE CONTEST
Grand Prize—$10,000
Gloria Bradley
Napierville, Illinois

2½ cups shredded sweetened coconut
1 cup unsalted macadamia nuts, chopped
1 (14-ounce) can sweetened condensed milk
1 teaspoon vanilla extract

20 Premium Saltine Crackers (any variety), finely crushed
2 egg whites
6 ounces semisweet chocolate, chopped and melted

Preheat the oven to 350 degrees.

Place the coconut and nuts on a 15½x10½x1-inch baking pan. Bake until lightly toasted, about 10 minutes, stirring frequently. Let cool. Leave the oven on.

In a large bowl, combine the condensed milk and vanilla. Stir in the coconut, nuts, and crushed crackers; blend well. Beat the egg whites until stiff, then gently fold into coconut mixture. Drop by rounded tablespoons onto a lightly greased baking sheet.

Bake for 12 to 14 minutes or until golden around the edges. Let cool completely. When cool, dip the cookie bottoms into the melted chocolate and place on waxed paper. Refrigerate until set.

Makes 36 macaroons

Macadamia Fudge Torte

37TH PILLSBURY BAKE-OFF CONTEST
$1,000,000 Grand Prize—Special Occasion Desserts Category

Kurt Wait

Redwood City, California

Kurt Wait

Redwood City, California

Kurt first served his million-dollar recipe, Macadamia Fudge Torte, at a staff meeting for the health care marketing group in which he is an analyst. A self-taught cook, Kurt won rave reviews from the tasters, who encouraged him to enter the Bake-Off. He credits ease of preparation and suitability for special or everyday use for the success of this recipe. His strong interest in ecology leads him to cite Maui as a favorite vacation destination due to its unique plants, animals, and geology. Kurt particularly enjoys sharing the kitchen with his son, who has already entered and won several contests.

Filling

⅓ cup low-fat sweetened condensed milk (not evaporated)

½ cup semisweet chocolate chips

Cake

1 package Pillsbury Moist Supreme Devil's Food Cake Mix

1½ teaspoons ground cinnamon

⅓ cup oil

1 (16-ounce) can sliced pears in light syrup, drained

2 eggs

⅓ cup chopped macadamia nuts or pecans

2 teaspoons water

Sauce

1 (17-ounce) jar butterscotch caramel fudge ice cream topping

⅓ cup milk

Preheat the oven to 350 degrees. Spray a 9- or 10-inch springform pan with nonstick cooking spray.

In a small saucepan, combine the filling ingredients. Cook over medium-low heat until the chocolate is melted, stirring occasionally.

In a large bowl, combine the cake mix, cinnamon, and oil; mix on low speed for 20 to 30 seconds or until crumbly (mixture will be dry).

Place the pears in a blender or food processor and blend until smooth.

In a large bowl, combine 2½ cups of the cake mix mixture with the pureed pears and eggs; beat on low speed until moistened. Beat 2 minutes on medium speed. Spread the batter evenly in the prepared pan. Drop the filling by spoonfuls over the batter. Stir the nuts and water into the remaining cake mix mixture. Sprinkle over the filling.

Bake for 45 to 50 minutes or until the top springs back when touched lightly in the center. Let cool 10 minutes. Remove the sides of the pan. Let cool 1½ hours or until room temperature.

In a small saucepan, combine the sauce ingredients. Cook over medium-low heat for 3 to 4 minutes or until well blended, stirring occasionally.

To serve, spoon 2 tablespoons warm sauce onto an individual serving plate; top with a wedge of the torte. If desired, serve with vanilla ice cream or frozen yogurt and garnish with chocolate curls.

Makes 12 servings

Caramel White Chocolate Cheesecake

T. MARZETTI'S CARAMEL APPLE DIP CONTEST
First Place
Edwina Gadsby
Great Falls, Montana

1¼ cups graham cracker crumbs

¼ cup sugar

½ teaspoon ground cinnamon

¼ cup (½ stick) margarine or butter, melted

2 (6-ounce) or 12 (1-ounce) packages white chocolate baking bars

½ cup heavy cream

2 (8-ounce) packages cream cheese, softened

4 eggs

1 tablespoon vanilla extract

1½ cups T. Marzetti's Old Fashioned Caramel Apple Dip

Preheat the oven to 300 degrees.

Combine the first four ingredients; press on the bottom of a 9-inch springform pan.

In a saucepan over low heat, melt 10 ounces of the white chocolate with the cream, stirring until smooth. Remove from the heat; let cool.

In a large mixer bowl, beat the cream cheese until fluffy; beat in the eggs one at a time until blended. Stir in the white chocolate mixture and vanilla. Remove 1 cup of the batter and mix with 1 cup of the caramel apple dip. Spoon the batters alternately over the crust; cut through with a table knife to marbleize. Bake 55 minutes or until set (center will be slightly soft). Turn off the oven; let the cake stand in the oven for 1 hour. Remove and let cool completely. Chill.

To make caramel white chocolate sauce, combine the remaining 2 ounces of white chocolate with the remaining ½ cup caramel apple dip in a small microwave-safe bowl. Microwave on high 40 seconds, stirring after 20 seconds to marbleize but not blend. Serve with the cheesecake. Store the cheesecake in the refrigerator.

Makes 16 servings

Peach Cake Supreme

MARTINI & ROSSI ASTI STATE OF DESSERT RECIPE CONTEST
First Place
Debbie Puette
Lilburn, Georgia

3 medium peaches, peeled, pitted, and cut into ½-inch slices

½ cup firmly packed brown sugar

¾ cup coarsely chopped pecans

¾ cup butterscotch morsels

4 ounces cream cheese, softened

2 eggs

⅓ cup unsalted butter, softened

¾ cup plus 2 tablespoons granulated sugar

¾ teaspoon vanilla extract

1¼ teaspoons baking powder

½ teaspoon salt

1½ cups sifted cake flour

½ cup plus 2 tablespoons milk

8 maraschino cherry halves

2 cups whipped topping

Preheat the oven to 350 degrees. Generously oil and flour a 9-inch cake pan.

Place the peach slices in the bottom of the prepared pan. Sprinkle with ¼ cup of the brown sugar, the pecans, and butterscotch morsels.

In a small bowl, beat the cream cheese on high speed until smooth. Gradually beat in 1 egg until smooth. Beat in the remaining ¼ cup brown sugar until thoroughly mixed. Pour over the peaches and set aside.

In a medium bowl, cream the butter and granulated sugar on low speed. On medium speed, beat in the remaining egg, vanilla, baking powder, and salt. Alternately beat in the flour and milk until thoroughly mixed, 6 to 7 minutes. Pour the mixture over the peaches. Bake 45 to 50 minutes or until the cake comes loose from the sides of the pan.

Let the cake cool in the pan for 15 minutes, then turn out onto a serving platter. You may have to put some peaches or other bits that remain in the pan back on the cake. Let cool completely. Decorate with maraschino cherries and whipped topping. Serve immediately.

Makes 6 servings

Key Lime-White Chocolate Cookies

BISQUICK RECIPE CONTEST
First Place—Desserts
Joni Hilton
Carmichael, California

½ cup (1 stick) margarine or butter, softened

¾ cup packed brown sugar

2 tablespoons granulated sugar

1 egg

1½ teaspoons vanilla extract

2⅓ cups Bisquick Original baking mix

6 drops green food color (optional)

1 (6-ounce) package white chocolate baking bars, cut into chunks

1 tablespoon grated lime zest

Preheat the oven to 350 degrees.

Beat the margarine, sugars, egg, and vanilla in a large bowl until well mixed. Stir in the baking mix. Stir in food color (if desired), white chocolate chunks, and lime zest.

Drop the dough by rounded teaspoonfuls onto an ungreased baking sheet. Bake 8 to 10 minutes or until set but not brown. Let cool 1 minute before removing from the baking sheet. Cool on a wire rack.

Makes about 3½ dozen cookies

Grenoble Tart

DARIGOLD'S "WHIP UP YOUR BEST" RECIPE CONTEST
First Place
Peggy Tirk
Seattle, Washington

1 cup all-purpose flour
⅓ cup Darigold Butter
¼ cup sugar
1 egg yolk

2 cups walnut halves
Caramel Sauce (recipe follows)
Darigold Whipping Cream, whipped
    and sweetened

Preheat the oven to 375 degrees.

Place the flour, butter, sugar, and egg yolk in a food processor and process until the dough holds together and forms a ball. Press the dough onto the bottom and sides of a 9-inch fluted tart pan with a removable bottom. Bake 10 to 12 minutes or until the edges turn light golden brown. Remove from the oven and let cool to room temperature. Fill the tart shell with the walnuts.

Prepare the Caramel Sauce and pour over the walnuts. Bake 10 minutes or until bubbly. Let cool thoroughly. Serve with a dollop of sweetened whipped cream.

Caramel Sauce

Combine ⅔ cup packed brown sugar, ¼ cup Darigold Butter, and ¼ cup dark corn syrup in a heavy saucepan and bring to a rapid boil over medium heat without stirring. Allow to boil for 1 minute *without stirring*. Remove from the heat; whisk in 2 tablespoons Darigold Whipping Cream. Pour immediately over the walnuts in the tart shell.

Makes 6 servings

Susan Moon's Apricot-Pineapple Pie

AMERICAN PIE COUNCIL ANNUAL NATIONAL PIE CHAMPIONSHIP
First Place—Amateur Fruit and Berry Category
Susan Moon
Denver, Colorado

Crust

2 cups all-purpose flour, sifted
¾ teaspoon salt
⅔ cup solid shortening (Crisco)
¼ cup cold water

Filling

1 cup quartered apricots
1 cup water
⅔ cup packed brown sugar
2 cups diced fresh ripe pineapple
1 teaspoon vanilla extract
1 tablespoon butter
Milk, as needed

To make the crust: Blend the flour with the salt. Cut in the shortening with a pastry blender (don't overdo it—clumps now will be flakes later). Sprinkle the water over the top while stirring and turning the mixture with your hands. Gather up the dough and coax it into 2 patties, working it lightly and lovingly. Refrigerate until ready to use.

To make the filling: Simmer the apricots in the water in a saucepan until tender, 20 to 30 minutes, stirring periodically to keep them from sticking. Add more water, a bit at a time, if needed to keep the mixture moist. Remove from the heat, stir in the brown sugar, and let cool. (You can do this step a day ahead of time and refrigerate overnight.)

Preheat the oven to 425 degrees.

Add the pineapple and vanilla to the apricot mixture and blend well. If the mixture seems too juicy, add 1 tablespoon of cornstarch dissolved in 2 tablespoons of pineapple juice. Turn the mixture into a pastry-lined 9-inch pie pan, dot the filling with butter, and rub the rim of the crust with milk. Cover with a vented top crust and press and crimp around the rim. Brush the top of the crust with milk. Bake for 20 to 25 minutes or until golden brown. Lower the oven temperature to 350 degrees and bake for 35 to 40 minutes more (1 hour total). Serve slightly warm.

Makes 8 servings

Marion Goldstein's Raspberry Silk Pie

AMERICAN PIE COUNCIL ANNUAL NATIONAL PIE CHAMPIONSHIP
First Place—Open Category
Marion Goldstein
Denver, Colorado

Cream Cheese Pie Crust (recipe follows), baked and cooled

Raspberry Layer

1 (10-ounce) package frozen raspberries with syrup, thawed
1 tablespoon cornstarch
1 tablespoon sugar
1 tablespoon Chambord (raspberry liqueur), optional
1 cup fresh raspberries

White Chocolate Layer

½ cup (1 stick) margarine or butter
⅓ cup sugar
4 ounces white chocolate (Tobler or Lindt preferred), melted
2 eggs

Finishing Touches

2 squares (2 ounces) semisweet chocolate, cut in pieces
2 tablespoons butter or margarine
10 fresh raspberries and mint leaves, for garnish

To make the raspberry layer: Puree the thawed raspberries in a blender or food processor; strain and discard the seeds. In a small saucepan, combine the cornstarch and sugar, blending very well. Slowly add the pureed raspberries and Chambord. Cook over low heat, stirring constantly, until thickened. Let the mixture cool, then spread over the crust. Arrange the fresh raspberries on top. Refrigerate.

To make the white chocolate layer: Beat the margarine or butter and sugar until light and fluffy. Gradually add the melted white chocolate, beating constantly. Add the eggs, one at a time, beating at the highest speed for 3 minutes after each addition. Pour over the raspberries and smooth the surface. Refrigerate.

In a small saucepan, melt the semisweet chocolate and 2 tablespoons butter. Stir well. Drizzle over the set white chocolate mixture. Garnish with fresh raspberries and mint leaves. Refrigerate at least 2 hours or longer to set.

To serve, let stand at room temperature 30 minutes or serve straight from the refrigerator.

Makes 10 servings

Cream Cheese Pie Crust

4   ounces cream cheese, at room temperature
4   ounces (1 stick) butter or margarine, softened

1   tablespoon sugar
1   cup all-purpose flour, sifted

Mix the cream cheese and butter well. Add the sugar and flour gradually, beating well with a mixer or in a food processor. Gather the dough and flatten into a disc. Put in a plastic bag and refrigerate at least 2 hours.

Remove the dough from the refrigerator 30 minutes prior to rolling it out. Roll dough on lightly floured surface into 12-inch round. Roll up on the rolling pin and gently unroll over a 10-inch tart pan with removable bottom or 10-inch springform pan. Pat into the bottom and up the sides of the pan and prick with a fork. Refrigerate for 15 minutes.

Preheat the oven to 450 degrees.

Bake the crust for 13 minutes. Reduce the oven temperature to 350 degrees and bake an additional 10 to 13 minutes. Remove from the oven when lightly browned and let cool.

Makes one 10-inch pastry shell

Triple Tropical Brownies

BAKER'S CHOCOLATE NATIONAL BEST BROWNIE RECIPE CONTEST
First Place—"Year Round Family Favorite"
Helen Conwell
Fairhope, Alabama

Brownie Layer

- **4** squares Baker's unsweetened baking chocolate
- **¾** cup (1½ sticks) butter or margarine
- **2** cups sugar
- **4** eggs
- **1** teaspoon vanilla extract
- **2** cups all-purpose flour
- **3** squares (3 ounces) Baker's semi-sweet baking chocolate, chopped

Banana Layer

- **¾** cup sugar
- **¼** cup (½ stick) butter or margarine
- **1** egg
- **1** tablespoon rum (optional)
- **1** cup all-purpose flour
- **½** teaspoon baking soda
- **1** medium banana, coarsely mashed
- **½** cup chopped toasted pecans
- **3** squares (3 ounces) Baker's premium white baking chocolate, chopped

Icing

- **1** cup confectioner's sugar
- **3** tablespoons butter or margarine, softened
- **2** tablespoons strong brewed coffee, at room temperature
- **1** square (1 ounce) Baker's semisweet baking chocolate, grated

Preheat the oven to 350 degrees. Line a 13x9-inch baking pan with foil and oil the foil.

To make the brownie layer: Microwave the unsweetened chocolate and butter in a large microwavable bowl on high 2 minutes or until the butter is melted. Stir until the chocolate is completely melted. Stir in the sugar, eggs, and vanilla until well blended. Stir in the flour and semisweet chocolate. Spread in the prepared pan.

To make the banana layer: Beat the sugar and butter in a medium bowl with an electric mixer on medium speed until light and fluffy. Beat in the egg and rum. Mix in the flour and baking soda. Stir in the bananas, nuts, and white chocolate. Spread carefully over the brownie batter. Bake 30 to 40 minutes or until a toothpick inserted in the center comes out with fudgy crumbs. Let cool in the pan.

To make the icing: Beat the confectioner's sugar, butter, and coffee in a medium bowl with an electric mixer on medium speed until smooth. Spread over the cooled brownies. Sprinkle with grated semisweet chocolate. Cut into squares.

Makes 24 brownies

Oatmeal Squares Snacker-Jax

8TH ANNUAL QUAKER OATMEAL "BAKE IT BETTER WITH OATS" RECIPE CONTEST

Best-of-Category Snack Mix

Betty Noel

Spokane, Washington

1 (16-ounce) box Quaker oatmeal squares cereal (regular or cinnamon flavor)	2 tablespoons dark corn syrup
1½ cups roasted Spanish peanuts	2 tablespoons molasses
½ cup (1 stick) margarine or butter	1 teaspoon salt (optional)
1 cup firmly packed brown sugar	1 teaspoon vanilla extract
	¼ teaspoon baking soda

Preheat the oven to 250 degrees. Line 2 baking sheets with waxed paper.

In a 13x9-inch baking pan, combine the oatmeal cereal squares and peanuts.

In a small saucepan, melt the margarine over medium heat. Stir in the brown sugar, corn syrup, molasses, and salt, if desired. Bring to a boil. Stir well. Boil 2 minutes without stirring. Remove from the heat. Add the vanilla and baking soda; mix well. Immediately pour over the cereal mixture; stir with a wooden spoon to evenly coat all pieces with the syrup mixture.

Bake 1 hour, stirring every 20 minutes. Transfer to the prepared baking sheets, spreading the mixture in an even layer. Let cool completely. Break into bite-size pieces. Store, tightly covered, at room temperature.

Makes 10 cups

Double Macadamia Crunch

SECOND ANNUAL MAUNA LOA MACADAMIA NUT CONTEST
Candy Category Winner
Diane Halferty
Tucson, Arizona

1   cup coarsely chopped Mauna Loa
    Macadamia Nuts
1   cup finely chopped Mauna Loa
    Macadamia Nuts
1   cup (2 sticks) butter

1⅓ cups sugar
1   tablespoon light corn syrup
3   tablespoons water
14 ounces milk chocolate, melted

Preheat the oven to 300 degrees. Spread the macadamia nuts in 2 shallow pans and toast in the oven, stirring occasionally, until delicately browned. Let cool.

Meanwhile, melt the butter over low heat in a heavy 2-quart saucepan. Add the sugar, corn syrup, and water. Cook, stirring occasionally, to the hard crack stage (300 degrees). Watch carefully after the candy reaches 280 degrees.

Quickly stir in the toasted coarsely chopped macadamia nuts. Spread in an ungreased 13x9x3-inch pan. Let cool.

Turn out onto waxed paper and spread the top with half the melted chocolate and sprinkle with half of the finely chopped macadamia nuts. Cover with waxed paper and turn over. Spread the candy with the remaining chocolate and sprinkle with the remaining nuts.

Refrigerate until the chocolate is firm. Break into pieces and enjoy.

Makes 2½ pounds

Millionaires Shortbread

Second Annual Mauna Loa Macadamia Nut Contest
Cookie Category Winner
Kay Cabrera
Waikoloa, Hawaii

Shortbread

- 2 cups all-purpose flour
- ½ cup confectioner's sugar
- ¼ teaspoon baking powder
- 1 cup (2 sticks) butter, slightly softened
- ½ teaspoon vanilla extract

Filling

- 1 pound unsalted macadamia nut halves and pieces
- 2½ cups granulated sugar
- ¾ cup heavy cream
- 7 ounces (2 sticks less 2 tablespoons) butter

Glaze

- ¾ cup heavy cream
- 3 ounces (1 stick less 2 tablespoons) butter
- ¼ cup light corn syrup
- 8 ounces bittersweet chocolate

Preheat the oven to 350 degrees.

To make the shortbread: Sift the flour, powdered sugar, and baking powder together into a medium bowl. Cut the butter into ½-inch pieces and rub into the dry mixture with the vanilla, working quickly and stopping when the ingredients hold together. Pat the dough evenly onto the bottom of a 13x9x2-inch baking pan. Prick evenly with a fork and bake about 20 minutes or until the edges are browned and the crust appears dry and crisp. Let cool (leave the oven on).

To make the filling: Spread the macadamia nuts on a baking sheet and lightly toast in the oven. Let cool (leave the oven on). Put the granulated sugar and just enough water to liquefy it into a heavy 2-quart saucepan. Set over high heat and boil rapidly until the sugar begins to caramelize. Swirl the pan gently to allow the caramel to color evenly, and continue to cook until it is a uniform mahogany brown. Pour all the cream in at once, standing back, as it will spatter and boil up. Remove the pan from the heat and swirl the mixture until the boiling subsides and it is evenly blended, then stir in the macadamia nuts. Let cool slightly, then spread over the shortbread base.

Set the pan on a baking sheet on the middle rack of the oven. Bake for about 17 minutes or until the caramel begins to bubble in the center. Remove and let cool completely.

To make the glaze: Bring the cream, butter, and corn syrup to a boil in a small heavy saucepan. Put the chopped bittersweet chocolate in a medium heatproof bowl and pour the cream mixture over it. Let stand for 5 minutes, then stir gently until the chocolate melts and blends evenly. Don't stir too fast or you will get bubbles that will mar the surface of the glaze. Pour the chocolate glaze onto the cooled caramel and tip the pan to spread it evenly. Let cool completely.

To serve, cut the cooled shortbread into squares. Store in the refrigerator.

Makes about 36 squares

A White Mercedes Birthday Cake

THE GREAT AMERICAN CHOCOLATE CONTEST
"It Takes the Cake" White Chocolate Special Award

Paula Anderson
Tierra Verde, Florida

½ cup water

4 ounces white chocolate, chopped into small pieces

1 cup unsalted butter, softened

2 cups granulated sugar

4 large eggs, separated

1 teaspoon vanilla extract

2½ cups sifted cake flour

½ teaspoon salt

1 teaspoon baking soda

1 cup buttermilk

White Chocolate Glaze

4 ounces white chocolate, chopped into small pieces for melting

¾ cup confectioner's sugar

⅛ teaspoon salt

2 tablespoons hot water

1 large egg yolk

2 tablespoons unsalted butter

½ teaspoon vanilla extract

Preheat the oven to 350 degrees. Line the bottom of three 8-inch cake pans with parchment or waxed paper and lightly oil the paper.

In a medium glass or microwave-safe bowl, boil the water in the microwave on high power. Add the white chocolate pieces and microwave for 2 minutes on defrost, stirring after 1 minute. Heat again and stir until the chocolate is completely melted. (White chocolate is temperamental, so be careful not to overcook or burn it.) Set aside to cool completely.

In a large bowl, cream the butter and sugar until fluffy. Add the egg yolks, one at a time, beating well after each addition. Add the cooled melted white chocolate and the vanilla and mix well.

In a separate bowl, sift together the cake flour, salt, and baking soda. In another bowl, beat the egg whites until they form stiff peaks.

Gradually add the sifted ingredients to the creamed butter mixture, alternating with the buttermilk and beating well after each addition. Gently fold in the egg whites.

Divide the batter among the prepared pans. Bake for 30 minutes or until a toothpick inserted in the center of the cakes comes out relatively clean. This cake is moist, so be careful not to overbake it. Let the cakes cool on wire racks for 5 minutes, then carefully remove them from the pans. Peel the waxed or parchment paper from the bottoms and let cool completely on the wire racks before frosting.

To make the white chocolate glaze: In a medium glass or microwave-safe bowl in the microwave, melt the white chocolate pieces for 2 minutes on defrost, stirring after 1 minute. Continue heating in this manner until the chocolate is fully melted. Set aside to cool completely.

Blend the confectioner's sugar, salt, and hot water into the cooled white chocolate. Add the egg yolk and beat well. Add the butter, 1 tablespoon at a time, beating thoroughly after each addition. Stir in the vanilla.

When the cakes are cooled, frost each layer with the glaze and set 1 layer on top of the next. This is a thin icing and should cover the cake lightly.

Makes 8 to 10 servings

Heavenly Crown

THE GREAT AMERICAN CHOCOLATE CONTEST
Prize Winner—Chocolate Tiramisu Mousse Trifle Category
Marjorie Ohrnstein
Los Angeles, California

16 ladyfingers, split in half
½ cup orange juice
6 ounces semisweet chocolate
1 cup firmly packed light brown sugar
3 large eggs, separated

1 (8-ounce) package cream cheese, softened
½ cup heavy cream
½ teaspoon vanilla extract
Chocolate shavings and whipped cream, for garnish (optional)

Using a pastry brush, lightly coat the cut sides of the ladyfingers with the orange juice. Place the cut sides down in a 9-inch springform pan, covering the bottom and sides.

Melt the chocolate. Set aside to cool completely.

In a large bowl, cream ½ cup of the brown sugar and the egg yolks. Add the cream cheese and mix well. Add the melted chocolate and stir to blend. Beat the heavy cream into the chocolate mixture until soft peaks form.

In a separate bowl, whip the egg whites with the vanilla and remaining ½ cup brown sugar, 1 tablespoon at a time, until firm peaks form. Gently fold the egg white mixture into the chocolate mixture.

Spoon the mousse into the springform pan on top of the ladyfingers. Smooth the top with a spatula and refrigerate for 6 to 12 hours. Remove the dessert from the refrigerator 30 minutes before serving. Garnish, if desired, with whipped cream and chocolate shavings.

Makes 12 servings

Cheatin' Fudge Brownie Cake

1992 QUAKER OATS "IT'S THE RIGHT THING TO DO"
RECIPE CONTEST
First Prize—Desserts/Cookies
Nancy Kalinowski
Claremont, California

¾ cup (5 ounces) packed pitted prunes

2 teaspoons vanilla extract

1 cup granulated sugar

½ cup skim milk

½ cup fat-free egg substitute, or 4 egg whites, slightly beaten

1 cup Quaker oats (quick or old-fashioned), uncooked

1 cup all-purpose flour

½ cup unsweetened cocoa powder

1 teaspoon baking soda

½ teaspoon salt (optional)

½ cup chopped nuts

2 tablespoons confectioner's sugar

Preheat the oven to 350 degrees. Spray 13x9-inch baking pan with nonstick cooking spray or oil lightly.

Place the prunes, 2 tablespoons water, and the vanilla in a blender or food processor. Blend on high or process until the prunes are finely chopped. Add 1 cup water; blend until almost smooth. Add the sugar, milk, and egg substitute; blend until smooth.

In a large bowl, combine the oats, flour, cocoa powder, baking soda, and salt, if desired; mix well. Add the prune mixture, mixing just until moistened. Stir in the nuts. Pour into the prepared pan. Bake 30 minutes or until the edges pull away from the sides of the pan. Let cool completely on a wire rack. Sprinkle with the confectioner's sugar. Store loosely covered.

Makes 16 servings

Strawberries in Mascarpone Cream

1993 CALIFORNIA STRAWBERRY FESTIVAL'S BERRY-OFF
Grand Prize Winner
Melody Favish
Oslo, Norway

Melody Favish

Oslo, Norway

Melody, who describes herself as a freelance traveler, certainly enjoyed the trip to California that she won in this contest. She also received a beautifully engraved silver tray at a black-tie gala. Even though Melody has lived overseas since around 1970, she has accumulated more than twenty wins. Her varied dining experiences no doubt contribute to her success. Since she is a part-time writer, much of her philosophy about food can be found in the many food articles she has written.

3 egg yolks
⅓ cup granulated sugar
½ teaspoon cornstarch
1 cup heavy cream
½ vanilla bean, split lengthwise
1 cup mascarpone cheese

8 cups perfectly ripe strawberries, hulled
½ cup light brown sugar (Demerara is best but hard to find)
½ cup almond-flavored liqueur
½ cup chopped pistachios or pine nuts

Beat the egg yolks with the granulated sugar and cornstarch until thick and lemon colored. Scald ½ cup of the cream with the vanilla bean. Let cool slightly.

Gradually beat the scalded cream into the egg yolk mixture. Pour into a saucepan and cook over medium heat, stirring constantly, until the mixture just reaches the boiling point. Remove from the heat immediately. Strain (to remove the vanilla bean) into a mixing bowl and set the bowl in a pan of cold water to cool. Stir often. When completely cool, beat in the mascarpone. Lightly whip the remaining cream and fold into the mascarpone mixture. Chill.

Clean the strawberries and halve lengthwise. About ½ hour before serving, sprinkle with all but 1 tablespoon of the sugar and liqueur. Stir to coat evenly. Cover and reserve.

If using pine nuts, toast in a nonstick pan without fat. Divide the strawberries among 6 flat plates or shallow soup bowls. Top with the mascarpone cream. Sprinkle with the remaining brown sugar. Drizzle with the remaining liqueur and top with the nuts.

Makes 8 servings

Texas Trail Riders

STAR COOKIE CONTEST
First Place
Jim Powell
Houston, Texas

1 cup granulated sugar

1 cup packed light brown sugar

½ cup butter or margarine, softened

½ cup butter-flavored shortening, softened

1½ cups quick-cooking oats

2 teaspoons vanilla extract

2 eggs, lightly beaten

2 cups all-purpose flour

1 teaspoon baking powder

1 teaspoon baking soda

1 cup semisweet chocolate chips

1 cup butterscotch chips

1 cup walnuts, chopped into pieces

8 ounces dates, chopped

Preheat the oven to 350 degrees. Spray a baking sheet with vegetable oil cooking spray.

With an electric mixer, cream both sugars with the butter and shortening in a large bowl until smooth. By hand, vigorously beat in the oats, vanilla, and eggs until well blended.

In a separate bowl, combine the flour, baking powder, and baking soda; mix well. Add half of the flour mixture to the butter mixture and blend well. Add the remaining flour mixture and blend well. From here on, use your hands to mix the dough.

Add the remaining ingredients and combine thoroughly with your hands. Form the dough into Ping-Pong size balls and place 2 inches apart on the prepared baking sheet; flatten slightly. Bake 10 to 12 minutes or until light brown. Let cool in the pan 1 to 2 minutes and place on racks to cool further. Store the cookies in an airtight container.

Makes 48 cookies

White Chocolate Magnolia Pecan Pie

1992 GEORGIA CRISCO PECAN PIE CONTEST

First Place

Mary Louise Lever

Rome, Georgia

Pastry Shell

1⅓ cups all-purpose flour

½ teaspoon salt

½ cup chilled Butter Flavor Crisco Shortening

3 tablespoons ice water mixed with 2 teaspoons vinegar

Filling

2 large eggs, beaten

1 (14-ounce) can sweetened condensed milk (not evaporated)

⅓ cup white crème de cacao liqueur (white chocolate liqueur)

2 teaspoons vanilla extract

4 ounces white baking chocolate, melted

⅓ cup butter, melted

3 tablespoons milk

½ teaspoon salt

2 cups chopped lightly toasted pecans

Pecan halves

To make the pastry: Combine the flour and salt; cut in the shortening. Add the water mixture, 1 tablespoon at a time as needed, tossing with a fork. Form into a ball. Wrap in plastic wrap, flattening the dough into a 5-inch round. Chill at least ½ hour. Roll out and place in a 9-inch pie plate. Finish the edges as desired. Chill in the freezer for at least ½ hour.

Preheat the oven to 425 degrees.

To make the filling: Combine all the ingredients except the pecans in a large bowl, blending well. Stir in the chopped pecans. Pour into the pie shell, topping with pecan halves placed side by side in a circle around the outer edge of the pie.

Bake 12 minutes; reduce the oven temperature to 350 degrees and bake 30 to 35 additional minutes or until set. Best served at room temperature or warm.

Makes 8 servings

Apple Yum-Yum Pie

WHITE LILY CORNMEAL RECIPE CONTEST
First Place—Desserts
Mrs. Jay H. Schablik
Maryville, Tennessee

1 cup White Lily Self-Rising Cornmeal Mix
1 cup quick-cooking oats
3 tablespoons sugar
1 teaspoon ground cinnamon
½ teaspoon ground nutmeg
½ cup butter or margarine, softened
1 (8-ounce) can yams or sweet potatoes, drained and mashed
1 teaspoon lemon juice
3 cups peeled, thinly sliced cooking apples (about 3 medium)
1 tablespoon light molasses
Ice cream or whipped cream (optional)

Preheat the oven to 350 degrees.

Combine the cornmeal mix, oats, sugar, cinnamon, nutmeg, and butter or margarine; mix until crumbly. Reserve ½ cup crumb mixture for topping. To the remaining crumb mixture add the yams and lemon juice; mix well. Spread the mixture over the bottom and up the sides of a 9-inch pie plate.

Place the apples in the crust; drizzle with the molasses. Sprinkle the reserved crumb mixture over the apples. Bake 25 to 30 minutes or until golden brown and the apples are tender. Serve warm or cold. Top with ice cream or whipped cream, if desired.

Makes 8 servings

Note: Two (20-ounce) cans of apple pie filling may be substituted for the sliced apples.

Maui Pine Cream Pie

1991–1992 CRISCO NATIONAL PIE BAKING COMPETITION
Grand Prize
Marian Ching
Hawaii

Pineapple Cream Filling

1 (20-ounce) can crushed pineapple (juice-packed or light syrup)
4 egg yolks, lightly beaten
1 tablespoon water
⅓ cup firmly packed cornstarch
1 cup granulated sugar
¼ teaspoon salt
2 cups milk
2 tablespoons butter or margarine
1 teaspoon vanilla extract

Pie Crust

1½ cups all-purpose flour
2 tablespoons granulated sugar
½ teaspoon salt
½ cup Butter Flavor Crisco Shortening
½ tablespoon finely chopped toasted unsalted macadamia nuts
2 teaspoons grated lemon zest
3 to 4 tablespoons cold milk

Cream Cheese Filling

1 (8-ounce) package cream cheese, softened
½ cup confectioner's sugar
½ teaspoon vanilla extract
⅓ cup finely chopped toasted unsalted macadamia nuts

Toppings

1 cup heavy cream, whipped, or 2 cups prepared whipped topping
1 teaspoon grated lemon zest
¼ teaspoon confectioner's sugar
Toasted finely chopped unsalted macadamia nuts

Optional Garnishes

1 slice canned pineapple, drained
Additional crushed pineapple, drained

To make the pineapple cream filling: Measure 1 cup drained pineapple. Reserve the remaining ⅓ cup pineapple for the cream cheese layer. Combine the egg yolks and water in a small bowl. Stir with a fork to blend. Stir in the cornstarch. Combine the sugar, salt, milk, and cup of pineapple in a medium saucepan. Cook and stir over medium heat (will appear curdled for a time) until the mixture almost comes to a boil. Reduce the heat to low. Add the egg yolk mixture slowly, stirring constantly. Cook and stir until thickened. Add the butter and vanilla. Remove from the heat. Cover the pan with waxed paper. Refrigerate 30 minutes or longer, stirring once or twice.

To make the crust: Combine the flour, sugar, and salt in a medium bowl. Cut in the Butter Flavor Crisco using a pastry blender (or 2 knives) until the mixture forms pea-size chunks. Add the nuts and lemon zest. Add the milk. Toss lightly with a fork until the dough will form a ball. Press between your hands to form a 5- to 6-inch "pancake." Wrap in waxed paper. Refrigerate 15 minutes.

Preheat the oven to 350 degrees. Flour the work surface and rolling pin lightly.

Roll the dough into a round 1 inch larger all around than an upside-down 9-inch pie plate. Loosen the dough carefully; fold into quarters. Unfold and press into the pie plate. Fold the edges under. Flute. Prick the bottom and sides thoroughly with a fork (50 times) to prevent shrinkage. Bake 15 to 20 minutes or until golden brown. Let cool completely.

To make the cream cheese filling: Combine the cream cheese and confectioner's sugar in a medium bowl. Beat with a fork until blended and smooth. Add the vanilla. Add the nuts and reserved ⅓ cup drained pineapple. Mix well. Spread the cream cheese filling over the bottom of the cooled baked pie shell. Cover with the pineapple filling.

To top, spread the pie with the whipped cream. Toss the lemon zest with the confectioner's sugar. Sprinkle the zest and nuts over the whipped cream. If desired, place a pineapple ring in the center of the topping. Sprinkle crushed pineapple pieces among the lemon zest and nuts.

Serve or refrigerate until ready to serve. Refrigerate leftovers.

Makes 8 servings

Pennsylvania Dutch Cake and Custard Pie

35TH PILLSBURY BAKE-OFF CONTEST
Grand Prize
Gladys Fulton
Summerville, South Carolina

Gladys Fulton

Summerville, South Carolina

Gladys began contesting in 1991 by winning South Carolina Electric and Gas' International Favorite Recipe for her Fettuccine with Spinach Sauce and Mandarin Oranges. The very next year she took the Grand Prize in the Pillsbury Bake-Off. In addition to contesting, Gladys keeps busy with volunteer work. One of her favorite activities is reading to children in elementary schools. When time permits, she also enjoys decorative crafts. Making jewelry is one of her specialties.

1 (15-ounce) package Pillsbury All Ready Pie Crusts

Filling
⅓ cup granulated sugar
2 tablespoons flour
1 teaspoon apple pie spice (see Notes)
1 cup applesauce
⅔ cup sour cream
⅓ cup molasses
1 egg, beaten

Cake
½ cup granulated sugar
¼ cup (½ stick) margarine or butter, softened
½ cup sour milk (see Notes)
1 egg
1 teaspoon vanilla extract
1¼ cups Pillsbury BEST All Purpose or Unbleached Flour (see Notes)
1 teaspoon baking powder
½ teaspoon salt
¼ teaspoon baking soda

Glaze

½ cup confectioner's sugar

2 tablespoons brewed coffee

Prepare pie crust according to package directions for a filled one-crust pie using a 9-inch pie pan or 9-inch deep-dish pie pan. (Refrigerate remaining crust for later use.)

Preheat the oven to 350 degrees.

To make the filling: In a medium bowl, combine the sugar, flour, and apple pie spice; mix well. Stir in the remaining filling ingredients; blend well. Set aside.

To make the cake batter: In a small bowl, combine the sugar and margarine; beat until well blended. Add the sour milk, egg, and vanilla; beat until smooth. Lightly spoon the flour into the measuring cups; level off. Add the flour, baking powder, salt, and baking soda to the batter; mix well. Spoon into the crust-lined pan. Carefully pour the filling mixture over the batter.

Bake 45 to 60 minutes or until the center springs back when touched lightly and the top is deep golden brown.

Meanwhile, in a small bowl, combine the glaze ingredients; blend well. Drizzle over the hot pie. Serve slightly warm.

Makes 8 to 10 servings

Notes: For the apple pie spice, you can substitute ½ teaspoon cinnamon, ¼ teaspoon ginger, ⅛ teaspoon nutmeg, and ⅛ teaspoon allspice. To make sour milk, add 1 teaspoon lemon juice to ½ cup milk; let stand 5 minutes. If using self-rising flour, omit the baking powder, salt, and baking soda.

Acknowledgments

It is a real dream come true to have all these wonderful recipes in one place, and it could not have been done without the cooperation and support of the fine companies that sponsor contests. Without exception, everyone who was approached about having their winning dish in this cookbook was enthusiastic about the idea. It is with heartfelt thanks that their willingness to share is acknowledged.

The Great American Meatloaf Contest gave permission to include Mexican Crock-Pot Meatloaf. This recipe was first printed in *The Great American Meatloaf Contest Cookbook* by T. K. Woods (Hearst Books, 1995).

The Great American Chocolate Contest gave permission to include Heavenly Crown and A White Mercedes Birthday Cake. These recipes were first printed in *The Great American Chocolate Cookbook* by T. K. Woods (Hearst Books, 1995).

The Stockton Asparagus Festival gave permission to include California Asparagus Salad.

The American Pie Council gave permission to include Marion Goldstein's Raspberry Silk Pie and Susan Moon's Apricot-Pineapple Pie.

Baker's Chocolate gave permission to include 3D Brownies and Triple Tropical Brownies.

Bays English Muffins gave permission to include Glazed Salmon Medallions, Majorcan Mushroom Tapas with Toasted Almond-Garlic Streusel, and Jumpin' Jack 'n' Pepper Pizzas.

Fetzer Wines gave permission to include Grilled Chicken Salad with Asian Ginger Dressing.

Bisquick gave permission to include Savory Pull-Apart Bread and Key Lime–White Chocolate Cookies.

Borden's Viva Light Butter gave permission to include Viva La Cinnamon Rolls and Garden Dinner Casserole.

The Catfish Institute gave permission to include Basil-Olive Pesto Stuffed Catfish, Ranchero Catfish, Spiced Rubbed Catfish Kabobs with Southwestern Salsa, and Orange Rosemary Poached Catfish Fillets.

Churny Feta Cheese gave permission to include Mediterranean Potato Salad.

Sonoma Dried Tomatoes gave permission to include Pasta Rags with Sonoma Tomato Cream Sauce and Spicy Crab Cakes with Chipotle Aioli.

Crisco gave permission to include White Chocolate Magnolia Pecan Pie and Maui Pine Cream Pie.

Craneberry's Inc. gave permission to include Glazed Shrimp with Fruit and Nutty Rice Pilaf, Craneberry's "Red Gold" Pork Roast, Pork Chops with Cranberry-Apple Stuffing and Sauce, and Cranberry Chicken Wings.

Darigold gave permission to include White Chocolate Strawberry Dream Pie, "Fried" Ice Cream Sundae, and Grenoble Tart.

The Pillsbury Company gave permission to include Macadamia Fudge Torte, Fudgy Bonbons, Pennsylvania Dutch Cake and Custard Pie, Creamy Broccoli and Wild Rice Soup, and Greek-Style Chicken and Pasta. Pillsbury, Bake-Off, Fast and Healthy, Rush Hour Recipes, and Green Giant are registered trademarks of The Pillsbury Company and are used with permission.

Southeastern United Dairy Industry Association gave permission to include Tortellini-Shrimp Wonderful.

The Delmarva Poultry Industry, Inc., gave permission to include Baked Chicken with Red-Peppered Onions and Chicken with Mushrooms and Sage Cream.

Eagle Brand Condensed Milk gave permission to include Fat-Free Peach Frozen Yogurt.

Del Monte Canned Fruits gave permission to include Del Monte Chicken 'n' Peaches Picante.

Family Circle and the Florida Citrus Growers gave permission to include Spicy Skillet Chicken, which was originally published in *Family Circle*.

The National Honey Board and *Family Circle* gave permission to include Honey Jalapeño Chicken with Tomato Olivada.

General Mills, Inc., gave permission to include Pork Chops Cubano, Smoky Chipotle Corn Bread, Venezuelan Mystery Pie, and Peppered Parmesan Bread-sticks. Fiber One is a registered trademark of General Mills. Red Band Flour, also a registered trademark, gave permission to include Charleston Four-Corner Biscuits.

The Gilroy Garlic Festival Association, a nonprofit private corporation, gave permission to include Sizzling Garlic and Citrus Shrimp. The recipe also appears in the *Gilroy Garlic Festival Cookbook*. The festival is held the last full weekend of July.

Gold Kist Farms and Gold Kist, Inc., gave permission to include Chicken-Broccoli Triangles, Basil-Crusted Chicken Oriental, Parisian Walnut-Dijon Chicken, and Chicken Salad with Cajun Dressing.

Johnson & Wales University gave permission to include Orzo-Stuffed Tenderloin with Herbed Crust and Sliced Potatoes Lyonnaise.

Martini & Rossi gave permission to include Peach Cake Supreme.

The California Strawberry Festival gave permission to include Antipasto Stuffed Strawberries, Strawberries in Mascarpone Cream, Very Berry Pork Chops, Spiced Strawberry-Glazed Roast Pork Tenderloin, and Thai'd and True Strawberry and Pasta Toss.

Kretschmer Wheat Germ gave permission to include Garlic-Crusted Tuscany

Burgers, Caribbean Crunch Snapper with Island Chutney, and Toasted Chicken Salad Wraps.

Mama Mary's Pizza Crust gave permission to include Sizzlin' Spicy Scampi Pizza and Apple Streusel Dessert.

Handi-Wrap gave permission to include Santa Fe–Shanghai Beef, Honey-Thyme Grilled Shrimp, and Steak Salad Supreme.

The Mauna Loa Macadamia Nut Corp. gave permission to include Double Macadamia Crunch, Mauna Loa Bread with Mac Nut Honey Butter, and Million-aires Shortbread.

T. Marzetti gave permission to include Caramel Ribbon Brownies and Caramel White Chocolate Cheesecake.

The National Pasta Association gave permission to include Hearty Fiesta Cassoulet.

The National Broiler Council, sponsor of The National Chicken Cooking Contest, gave permission to include Chicken Picante, Caribbean Chicken Drums, Baked Spicy Pineapple Balinese Chicken, Gingered Jamaican Jerk Chicken, Yucatan Chicken with Peach-Avocado Salsa, and Caribbean Chicken Fajitas.

The National Turkey Federation gave permission to include Lemon Turkey Stir-Fry with Pasta, Quick Turkey Appetizers, Deep-Dish Mediterranean Turkey Pizza, Chili Turkey 'n' Sweet Potato Stew, and Thai Turkey Toss.

Paul Newman's Own and Good Housekeeping gave permission to include Lasagna Primavera, Chicken Breasts Diavolo, and Tasty Thai Shrimp and Sesame Noodles.

Noilly Prat and the International Association of Culinary Professionals gave permission to include Noilly Prat Napoli Baked Shrimp.

Star magazine and Jim Powell gave permission to include Texas Trail Riders.

Quaker Oats gave permission to include Italian Pesto Oat Rolls, Oatmeal Squares Snacker-Jax, Cran-Apple Oatmeal Swirl Rolls, Cheatin' Fudge Brownie Cake, Italian Herbed Oatmeal Focaccia, Maple Pecan Oatmeal Bars, North Country Rosemary Olive Scones, Peanut Butter 'n' Fudge Filled Bars, and Tropical Lime Oat Bars.

Swift-Eckrich Butterball gave permission to include Pecan-Stuffed Turkey Breasts with Asparagus.

Ziploc gave permission to include Barbados Grilled Pork with Pineapple Salsa.

Woman's Day gave permission to include Cheese Ravioli–Asparagus Pie, Easy and Elegant Beef Stroganoff, and Grilled Salmon Steaks with Ginger-Chive Sauce.

The Lipton Company gave permission to include Pizza-Style Tortilla Stack.

The South Carolina Beef Board gave permission to include Peppered Sesame Beef Strips with Artichoke Hearts.

Sargento Cheese, sponsor of the Sargento "Cheese Makes the Recipe" contest, gave permission to include Quick Cheese Date Nut Scones, Mexican Chicken Cheese Soup Ranchero, Moroccan Cheddar Couscous, Garden Fresh Florentine, Classic Cheddar Corn, Scallops Olé, and Very Cheddar Cranberry Muffin Tops.

The Steel Packaging Council gave permission to include Tuscan Tuna and White Bean Bruschetta, Best-of-the-Border Three-Bean Dip, and Olivita Crostini.

The Veal Committee of the National Cattlemen's Beef Association gave permission to include Veal Saté with Peanut Sauce, Grilled Veal Chops with Fresh Fruit Salsa, Citrus-Rubbed Veal Chops with Sunshine Salsa, and Mediterranean Veal Burgers.

The Watkins Company gave permission to include Royal Pork Medallions.

The Wisconsin Cattlewomen's Association, sponsor of the World Beef Exposition, gave permission to include Mexican Beef and Barley Soup and Beef Tenderloin Mexicana.

Wesson Oil gave permission to include Extra-Crisp Cilantro-Crusted Fried Chicken.

White Lily Foods gave permission to include Apple Yum-Yum Pie and Key West Black-Eyed Pea Cakes.

Premium Saltines gave permission to include Baked Tomato Chowder and Maui Macadamia Macaroons.

The South Carolina Sweet Potato Board and Rosemary Whitlock gave permission to include Rocky Top Sweet Potato Casserole.

The National Oyster Cook-Off, held each year in Leonardtown, Maryland, gave permission to include Curried Oyster Stew, Baked Brie with Oysters 'n' Pistachios, Popeye's Oysters and Spinach with Bacon Bits, and Oyster Bruschetta "Roma."

Interbake Corporation gave permission to include Heaven Scent-sations and Chocolate Marshmallow Sandwich Bars.

The Mushroom Council gave permission to include Marinated Mushroom Salad with Italian Salsa and Gorgonzola Croutons, Kaleidoscope Mushroom Salad, and Mushroom-Stuffed Brie Baked en Croute.

Best Foods, makers of Hellmann's real mayonnaise, gave permission to include Waikiki Turkey Sandwich, Southwestern Chicken Sandwiches, and White Bean and Bacon Bruschettas.

The American National Cattlewomen, sponsor of The National Beef Cook-Off, gave permission to include Pronto Spicy Beef and Black Bean Salsa, Spanish Steak Roll with Sautéed Vegetables, Grecian Skillet Rib-Eyes, Oriental Short Rib Barbecue, and Pacific Rim Glazed Flank Steak.

Appendix

For those who may be new to cooking contesting, I have included the rules from three of the most important contests in the country. Of course, the dates change, and sometimes the "mail to" address does as well. If you read the rules carefully, though, even a novice can begin to see how to enter and win. The rules are repeated here just as taken from the pages of *The Cooking Contest Newsletter.*

Pillsbury Quick & Easy Bake-Off Contest

Deadline: Entries must be marked on or before October 18, ———, and received on or before midnight October 22, ———. To enter electronically, go to www.bakeoff.com and submit your recipe using the online entry form. All electronic entries must be received by 11:59 P.M. CDT on October 18, ———. Electronic entries should be submitted only once.

Prizes:

> (1) Grand Prize—$1,000,000
> (1) winner—GE Performance Kitchen
> (3) winners—$10,000
> (12) winners—$2,000
> 100 finalists win a trip to San Francisco, CA, along with $100
>   expense money and a new GE Advantium Oven.

Categories: *Easy Weeknight Meals*—Easy-to-make main dishes, such as casseroles, skillet meals, soups, sandwiches and salads, that meet one of the following criteria: (1) ingredients can be prepared and assembled in 15 minutes or less (not counting cooking or baking time), or (2) recipe can be completely prepared and ready to serve in 30 minutes or less.

Yummy Vegetables—Fast and flavorful vegetable side dishes and salads.

Fast & Fabulous Desserts & Treats—Family-pleasing desserts and treats, such as cookies, bars, muffins, coffee cakes and pies, that are prepared in 15 minutes or less (not counting baking, cooking or cooling time).

Casual Snacks & Appetizers—Savory (not sweet) snacks and appetizers that are prepared with no more than 7 ingredients (not including water, plain salt and ground pepper).

How to Enter: Send in your best original recipe that uses at least one of the required products listed on the Entry Form in the quantity specified. On the Entry Form or on plain paper, print or type your name, address, telephone number, e-mail address, store where you purchased your ingredients, and the grocery stores where you regularly shop, and check the eligible product(s) used in your recipe and the Recipe Category you are entering. On a separate 8.5" x 11" white or light-colored sheet, print or type this same information and your recipe. List every recipe ingredient (including garnishes) with exact measurements and complete directions. Enter as many recipes as you'd like. Be sure to include an Entry Form for each recipe submitted. To enter by postal mail, **mail to:** The Pillsbury Bake-Off Contest, Dept. B, PO Box 5704, Hopkins, MN 55343.

Rules: 100 finalists will win trips to San Francisco, CA, February 26–29, ——, to compete for 16 cash prizes totaling $1,054,000. Trip includes round-trip economy coach transportation for finalist from major commercial airport nearest finalist's home, hotel accommodations for three nights at the Marriott Hotel, all meals, $100 expense money, and a new GE Advantium Oven (total estimated retail value with installation: $1,500). One top winner will be chosen in each of the four Recipe Categories: Easy Weeknight Meals; Yummy Vegetables; Fast & Fabulous Desserts & Treats; and Casual Snacks & Appetizers. One of these Category winners will be selected as the $1 million Grand Prize Winner; the three remaining Category winners will each receive $10,000. In addition, three $2,000 prizes will be awarded in each of the four Recipe Categories. The final judging panel will award the GE Innovation Award to a non-cash-winning finalist for the recipe the panel deems the most innovative. The GE Innovation Award winner will receive a GE Profile Performance Kitchen, which consists of a Range, Refrigerator, Microwave, Dishwasher and Compactor (total estimated retail value: $5,000). The $1 Million Grand Prize will be awarded as an annuity payable at $50,000 each year for 20 years, no interest, with the first payment payable February 29, ——, and the final payment February 28, ——. Prize not transferable. All taxes and other expenses, if any, are the sole responsibility of the winners. This contest is void where prohibited or otherwise regulated.

Use of automated processes and devices to submit electronic entries is not permitted. Pillsbury is not responsible for any changes or effects caused to the entrant's computer system as a result of submitting electronic entries. All entries must be submitted via the US Postal Service or the web site electronic form. No entries will be accepted via facsimile or other express delivery services. No responsibility can be assumed for lost, late, misdirected, damaged or postage-due mail, or to entries that cannot be processed due to phone, network, electronic or computer hardware or software failure, or technical failures of any kind. In the case of duplicate recipes, the first entry received will be judged. If you wish acknowledgment of your entry, include a SASE with your entry. By submitting your recipe, you accept all contest rules and agree to be bound by the decisions of the judges, which will be final. You also agree that your recipe becomes the property of Pillsbury, and Pillsbury reserves the right to edit, adapt, copyright, publish and use any or all of them, without compensation. All entries must be quick and easy and meet the requirements of the Category entered.

If you are one of the 100 finalists, you will be notified by December 15, ———. Finalists will be required to sign an affidavit of eligibility and a liability release within 7 days of notification. In the event of noncompliance with this requirement, a finalist may forfeit prize and an alternate finalist will be selected. As a finalist, you will be invited to San Francisco, CA, where you must prepare your recipe yourself, exactly as submitted, for final judging between 8:00 A.M. and 1:00 P.M. PST on February 28, ———. Except where prohibited by law, each finalist will be required to sign a release giving Pillsbury and its nominees full rights to use the finalist's name and likeness for Bake-Off Contest–related advertising and publicity. Pillsbury and GE will select and supply the ingredients and cooking equipment to be used during preliminary judging and at the final Bake-Off competition. Where possible, those items will be products of Pillsbury and GE.

Eligibility: You are eligible if you are 10 years of age or older on October 18, ———, and are a resident of the United States or Puerto Rico. You are not eligible to enter and will be disqualified if: (1) You are a food professional, such as a chef, food writer or food home economist who creates recipes for pay. (2) You, your spouse, your parent or your child (all regardless of present place of residence) or anyone currently living in your household has been a finalist in three or more Bake-Off Contests, or has previously been a Bake-Off Grand Prize Winner. (3) You are: an employee of The Pillsbury Company or its subsidiaries and affiliated food companies or its agencies; an employee of GE Appliances, its subsidiaries, affiliates, or agencies; or a member of the immediate household of such employees. Anyone living in the household of a Pillsbury employee working at its corporate headquarters or consumer food locations as well as said employee's spouse, parents, and children are also ineligible.

Judging: Recipes will be judged for: (1) taste and appearance; (2) consumer appeal; (3) creativity; and (4) appropriate use of eligible products. Initial judging will be done by a professional judging agency and home economists. Entries must be newly created and the original recipe of the contestant. Judges will disqualify previously published recipes, such as those in major cookbooks, in magazines, from food companies and winners in national contests, unless the recipe features changes considered significant by the judges. Each finalist will be required to certify, on information or belief, that his or her recipe has not been published or publicized and has not won a national contest. Judges reserve the right to assign entries to the Recipe Category they deem appropriate. Final judging will be done by consumer research and a panel of food experts.

Deadline: Postmarked by October 15, ———

Prizes:

> First Place—$25,000
> Second Place—$5,000
> Third Place—$3,000
> Fourth Place—$2,000
> Fifth Place—$1,000

Categories: Chicken dishes

How to Enter: Write your name, address and phone number on first page of each recipe. Enter as many recipes as you like but each must be on a separate sheet of paper. Entries must be original. "Original" is defined as not previously published in the same or substantially the same form. Contest finalists will be required to certify that the recipe entry is original. Chicken recipes may be mailed, sent electronically or faxed to: Chicken Contest, Box 28158, Washington, DC 20038-8158. Fax: 202-293-4005. Website: www.eatchicken.com.

Rules: Chicken is the only required ingredient for recipes and can be prepared whole, in parts or in any combination of parts. Recipe preparation and ingredients are only limited by the imagination and creativity of the entrants. However, all recipes must be original, make 4–8 servings and take less than 3 hours to complete. Please, no Duck Confits.

Entries will not be acknowledged or returned. Taxes on prizes are the responsibility of winners. All entries become the property of National Chicken Cooking Contest. Entry constitutes permission to edit, modify, adapt, publish and otherwise use the recipe in any way without compensation.

One finalist representing each state and the District of Columbia will be selected by an independent recipe judging agency, not by random drawing. Fifty-one contestants will win an expense-paid trip to the 43rd National Cook-Off in Dallas, Texas. The cook-off date is May 14, ——— and will be at the Hyatt Regency Hotel in Dallas, Texas.

Eligibility: A finalist is selected from each state and the District of Columbia. Directors and employees of National Broiler Council and their immediate families are not eligible, nor are previous first-place winners.

Judging: Judging will be based on: Taste, Appearance, Simplicity and Appeal. A panel of national magazine and newspaper food editors and other well-known food experts will participate in the final judging.

Ninth Annual Newman's Own & Good Housekeeping Recipe Contest

Deadline: Posted by July 15, ――――

Prizes: Grand Prize—$50,000 donated to the charity of your choice.

Seven finalists, as well as the finalist from the food professional category, will each have $10,000 donated to the charity of choice. Also, the store named on the entry form of the Grand Prize winner will have $10,000 donated to its favorite charity. The stores named by the remaining eight finalists will each have $7,500 donated to their charities of choice. Selection of the charity to receive the award will be made by the chief executive officer of each retailer.

Sixteen runner-up charity awards of $5,000 each will be awarded as follows: Two will be awarded in each finalist category, with the exception of the food professional's category.

Categories: Only appetizer, main-dish, or dessert recipes using one of the specified Newman's products will be considered.

1. Salad Dressing (Olive Oil & Vinegar, Caesar, Balsamic Vinaigrette, Ranch, Light Italian, Parisienne Dijon Lime, or Family Recipe Italian)
2. Pasta Sauce (Marinara, Marinara with Mushrooms, Sockarooni, "Say Cheese," Bombolina, Diavolo, or Roasted Garlic with Red & Green Peppers)
3. Salsa (Mild, Medium, Hot, Roasted Garlic, Peach, or Pineapple)
4. Popcorn (Microwave Natural, Butter Flavor, Natural Light, Light Butter, or popcorn in jars)
5. Newman's Own Organics Chocolate (Sweet Dark Chocolate, Milk Chocolate, Milk Chocolate with Rice Crisps, Espresso Sweet Dark Chocolate, Sweet Dark Chocolate with Orange Oil, and Milk Chocolate Butter Toffee Crunch)

How to Enter: You may enter only one recipe per category, and each recipe entry must be typed or printed in ink on an 8.5" x 11" piece of plain white paper and mailed with the completed entry form. Entries should be sent by first-class mail only to: Newman's Own, Inc./Good Housekeeping Recipe Contest, P.O. Box 8010, Westport, CT 06888.

Rules: Recipes must be original and previously unpublished. Entries must include standard U.S. measurements, a complete list of ingredients in order of use, complete preparation directions, pan sizes, timing, temperature, number of servings, and other relevant information. Ingredients must be readily available. All entries become the property of Newman's Own, Inc., and Good Housekeeping and will not be returned. Sponsors are not responsible for lost or misdirected mail.

Each of the nine finalists and a traveling companion will receive a trip to New York City, consisting of: round-trip air travel via American Airlines from the airport nearest the winner's home; a two-night stay at The Waldorf-Astoria, New York; and $1,000 to cover any miscellaneous expenses. The ARV is $3,000. All nine finalists will lunch with Paul Newman at the renowned Waldorf-Astoria, where the chef will prepare the finalists' recipes, not including the food professional's entry. These eight dishes will be served to Paul Newman, and he will select the Grand Prize winner. The trip and the final judging will take place in October ———. Should a finalist be unable to make the trip at the time established by the sponsor, an alternate finalist will be selected.

All charities selected for donation must be bona fide charitable organizations with proper IRS exemption, and approved by Paul Newman. By submitting an entry, entrant agrees to the use of his or her name, photo, and recipe submission in any form for publicity or trade purposes by Newman's Own, Inc., and by Good Housekeeping without any additional compensation. Newman's Own, Inc. and Good Housekeeping have the right to adapt, modify, edit, and publish recipes as they deem fit.

Any local, state, or federal taxes are the responsibility of the winners. There are no substitutions of prizes as offered except at the discretion of the sponsors. Prizes are not transferable. Winners will be notified by mail no later than September 1, ———, and will be required to sign and return within 14 days of receipt an Affidavit of Eligibility, Publicity, Liability, and Ownership Release. Travel companions will be required to sign a liability release.

WINNERS' LIST: send an SASE before October 1, ———, to: Winner's, Newman's Own, Inc./Good Housekeeping Recipe Contest, P.O. Box 8010, Westport, CT 06888.

Eligibility: The contest is open to any resident of the United States 18 years or older. The contest is also open to a class (any grade) of children or a youth organization. Previous contest finalists, as well as employees of Newman's Own, Inc., the Hearst Corporation, their affiliates, promotional agencies, and families are not eligible to enter.

Judging: Entries will be judged equally on the basis of taste, visual presentation, originality, and ease of preparation. Preliminary judging will be done by the Good Housekeeping Institute's Food Department. Nine finalists will be selected from the following nine categories: one from each of the five product categories (salad dressing, pasta sauce, salsa, popcorn, and chocolate); one from a multi-product usage category; one from an organized group (either a recipe from an individual belonging to a group, or a recipe that has been developed by the group as a whole); one from a school class or youth organization; and one from an individual professionally involved in the preparation of food for pay, such as a chef, home economist, food writer, or culinary student. All of the entries must use one of the above-referenced Newman's Own products in the recipes.

How to Subscribe

If you would like to join the cooks who already enjoy *The Cooking Contest Newsletter*, you can receive twelve monthly editions by sending $19.95 to:

The Cooking Contest Newsletter
P. O. Box 339
Summerville, South Carolina 29484

Index